Children, Teachers and Learning Series
Series Editor: Cedric Cullingford

Children's Thinking

Titles in the *Children, Teachers and Learning* series

Children's Thinking

Promoting Understanding in the Primary School

Michael Bonnett

CASSELL

Cassell

Villiers House   387 Park Avenue South
41/47 Strand   New York, NY 10016–8810
London WC2N 5JE

First published 1994

British Library Cataloguing-in-Publication Data
A catalogue record for this book is available from the British Library.

Library of Congress Cataloging-in-Publication Data
Applied for.

ISBN 0–304–32939–8 (hardback)
    0–304–32937–1 (paperback)

Typeset by Colset Private Limited, Singapore
Printed and bound in Great Britain by
Biddles Ltd, Guildford and King's Lynn

Contents

Contents

To Sandy

Acknowledgements

I am indebted to many people for the opportunities they have given to discuss the issues presented in this book, but I owe a particular debt of gratitude to Charles Bailey, David Bridges and Trisha Dale for their encouragement and helpful comments on an early draft.

Foreword

The books in this series stem from the conviction that all those who are concerned with education should have a deep interest in the nature of children's learning. Teaching and policy decisions ultimately depend on an understanding of individual personalities accumulated through experience, observation and research. Too often in recent years decisions on the management of education have had little to do with the realities of children's lives, and too often the interest shown in the performance of teachers, or in the content of the curriculum, has not been balanced by an interest in how children respond to either. The books in this series are based on the conviction that children are not fundamentally different from adults, and that we understand ourselves better by our insight into the nature of children.

The books are designed to appeal to *all* those who are interested in education and who take it as axiomatic that anyone concerned with human nature, culture or the future of civilization is interested in education – in the individual process of learning, as well as what can be done to help it. While each book draws on recent findings in research and is aware of the latest developments in policy, each is written in a style that is clear, readable and free from the jargon that has undermined much scholarly writing, especially in such a relatively new field of study.

Although the audience to be addressed includes all those concerned with education, the most important section of the audience is made up of professional teachers, the teachers who continue to learn and grow and who need both support and stimulation. Teachers are very busy people, whose energies are taken up in coping with difficult circumstances. They deserve material that is stimulating, useful and free of jargon and is in tune with the practical realities of classrooms.

Each book is based on the principle that the study of education is a discipline in its own right. There was a time when the study of the principles of learning and the individual's response to his or her environment was a collection of parts of other disciplines – history, philosophy, linguistics, sociology and psychology. That time is assumed to be over and the books address those who are interested in the study of children and how they respond to their environment.

Each book is written both to enlighten the readers and to offer practical help to develop their understanding. They therefore not only contain accounts of what we understand about children, but also illuminate these accounts by a series of examples, based on observation of practice. These examples are designed not as a series of rigid steps to be followed, but to show the realities on which the insights are based.

Most people, even educational researchers, agree that research on children's learning has been most disappointing, even when it has not been completely missing. Apart from the general lack of a 'scholarly' educational tradition, the inadequacies of such study come about because of the fear of approaching such a complex area as children's inner lives. Instead of answering curiosity with observation, much educational research has attempted to reduce the problem to simplistic solutions, by isolating a particular hypothesis and trying to improve it, or by trying to focus on what is easy and 'empirical'. These books try to clarify the real complexities of the problem, and are willing to be speculative.

The real disappointment with educational research, however, is that it is very rarely read or used. The people most at home with children are often unaware that helpful insights can be offered to them. The study of children and the understanding that comes from self-knowledge are too important to be left to obscurity. In the broad sense real 'research' is carried out by all those engaged in the task of teaching or bringing up children.

All the books share a conviction that the inner worlds of children repay close attention, and that much subsequent behaviour and attitudes depend upon the early years. They also share the conviction that children's natures are not markedly different from those of adults, even if they are more honest about themselves. The process of learning is reviewed as the individual's close and idiosyncratic involvement in events, rather than the passive reception of, and processing of, information.

Cedric Cullingford

Preface

The intention of this short book is to make accessible to students, teachers and others concerned with the education of children in the primary age range some work in philosophy and philosophy of education on the nature of thinking and understanding. The topics of thinking and how best to promote understanding clearly lie at the heart of any worthwhile conception of education and human development, and one of the effects of introducing the National Curriculum has been to provoke a wide ranging reappraisal of them. But what exactly is involved in the development of thinking, and what is the role of the teacher in facilitating it? The pursuit of these questions leads to further ones such as:

What is it to think, and to understand?

Are there significantly different kinds of thinking and understanding, and if so what is their value?

How can we help children to 'think for themselves'?

How do thinking and understanding relate to conscious life as a whole, behaviour, and our ways of relating to others and the world in general?

Like anyone else who makes curriculum proposals, the authors of the National Curriculum make many assumptions regarding these questions, but perhaps in the interests of political expediency and achieving quick consensus they have often preferred to leave them tacit and unexamined. To this extent their proposals remain unclear and unargued, possible errors and inconsistencies remaining undetected. But to those who really care about the truth and about how best to interpret and implement the National Curriculum in the educational interests of the children in their care – and, equally as important, about how to help the Curriculum evolve in ways that are educationally desirable – they are questions that have to be acknowledged and pursued. Such questions form the focus of this book. They will lead us into fundamental issues concerning the nature of meaning in its different forms, and the kind of education needed to allow individuals to develop qualities of freedom and responsibility needed by a democratic society. It will be argued that no matter what the stage of our involvement with the development of children, to contribute responsibly we must have a better than average awareness of the possibilities of human development as a whole and the world into which we are giving children entrance, and in which they must take up their place. No doubt some of the issues involved are difficult, but I cannot but think that to shirk them – to simply follow other people's prescriptions unthinkingly – is to do a grave disservice to the children in our care, particularly when, as we shall see, certain aspects of the National Curriculum and possibilities of implementing it are so seriously flawed.

Yet the overarching purpose of this book is not essentially to evaluate any one set of curriculum proposals however prominent they may be at this time. It does not aspire to be 'current' in this sense and I have not felt constrained to give a survey of a wide range of the latest research and discussion that might be held by some to have a bearing on the issues under debate. On the contrary, this has been deliberately eschewed to a large extent as it seems to me that such an emphasis is both unnecessary and undesirable. The key issues in the area are longstanding and are appreciated more through systematic reflection than through the acquisition of myriad research findings – whose common effect is to discourage rather than stimulate thinking and understanding. What is required is not yet more 'evidence', but to perceive the significance of what we often already know.

For those who have little or no previous involvement with a philosophical approach to issues, some of the views, ideas and names listed in the Contents and Bibliography may appear daunting. Such apprehension is understandable in the light of popular conceptions of philosophy that depict it as unduly 'heavy' and academic in the sense of being abstracted from the real concerns of life. But this conception is largely a caricature. Philosophy and philosophers proper have always been concerned with issues that lie at the heart of human consciousness and are readily recognizable as such by those who are prepared to reflect on such issues for themselves. It is a central aspiration of this book to introduce some relevant thinkers and ideas in a way that makes clear their essential contribution to the topic of developing children's thinking and understanding in the primary school. This will be done by relating their views to familiar situations and ideas, and illustrating how these views can enlarge and refine our understanding of them.

Yet it is important to recognize that the initial approach to some of the underlying issues involved is not *always* best made from the perspective of the child in primary school. Sometimes the first important step is to recognize the issues and claims in terms of one's own experience and to appreciate the essential continuity of this with the experiences of children. Alongside the many beneficial effects of the work of influential psychologists such as Piaget and Kohlberg, who have encouraged us to take seriously the structure of children's thinking in its own right, is the danger that their focus on ways in which children's thinking at different stages may differ from that of adults may lead us to see children as a species apart. Beside the obvious dangers of 'stage' stereotyping, such an orientation can be generally unhelpful and is often palpably untrue when it comes to understanding the more fundamental human motives and aspirations which inform thinking and its development. Consequently, the stance sometimes taken in this book will be to invite readers to consult their own experience and understanding as a prerequisite to considering how best to promote that of children.

Part One
Thinking and Understanding in the Context of the Primary School Curriculum

CHAPTER 1
Introduction: What's the Problem?

It perhaps borders on the truistic to say that one of the central features that we have in mind when we speak of the development of a person is the development of his or her capacity to think and to understand. It is largely in terms of these capacities that, for example, we assess individuals' ability to take responsibility for their actions and their lives, cope with new situations, move on to the next challenge or contribute to a demanding enterprise. Indeed, it is largely in terms of the quality of their thinking and understanding that we judge their intelligence, their overall level of maturity, and sometimes their worth. Those who can't or don't think about situations in which they find themselves, or whose thinking is confused or chaotic, are ill-equipped to deal with life and in extreme cases would normally be put into care.

Thus, we don't have to go quite as far as Descartes' famous dictum 'I think, therefore I am' to recognize the centrality to human being of the capacity to think. And it is not surprising that amongst primary teachers at least – if not some politicians – it has become a commonplace now to denigrate in education the mere learning up of facts and theories, mechanical skills and other people's views. Rather teachers claim to seek to develop *understanding* of what is learnt; they want children to *think* about what they are doing, indeed they want them to *think for themselves*.

Without this underlying philosophy much current practice in primary schools would make no sense. The moves in mathematics teaching over the last three decades are a case in point. In 'modern maths' the emphasis has been placed upon the development of mathematical literacy: a grasp of mathematical ideas and concepts – the 'language' of mathematics – as against prowess in mechanical computation exercises. Similarly, the emphasis in the teaching of reading and writing has come to focus on gaining and communicating meaning, articulating one's own thoughts and ideas, expressing oneself and understanding the expressions

3

of others.[1] And what is true for the 'three Rs' is even more true for many other areas of the curriculum, such as art, music, drama, project-work or science, where first-hand research, experiment and discovery, discussion and the relatively free exchange of ideas are frequently advocated. Much of what currently goes on in schools would have to be regarded as at best inefficient, and at worst a scandalous waste of time, if the simple accumulation of stocks of facts and mechanical skills was the overriding concern of education. And this, of course, is precisely the criticism that many traditionalist spectators of education have been making with increasing vociferousness. They claim that under the influence of 'progressivism' education has indeed lost its way and that there is a pressing need to return to more didactic teaching aimed at clearly specified and measurable goals – a theme embraced by the authors of the National Curriculum.

On the one hand, then, there seems to be implicit in much recent practice a claim that certain approaches to teaching and learning are justified because they develop children's thinking and understanding. On the other hand, there is the vigorously pressed counter-claim that much of what has happened over recent decades in primary schools has been thoroughly misguided and has led to a serious decline in educational standards. How are we to assess such competing claims? And if it turned out that so-called progressive approaches to teaching were justified in terms of the quality of thinking and understanding they enabled pupils to develop, should education be given this sort of emphasis anyway?

It could be, and has been, objected that there is more to the full development of a person than the development of thinking and understanding. What of other facets of personal development, such as the emotions, moral sensitivity, good habits and general character formation? Also, is there not a large body of practical skills and sheer factual knowledge that a person needs simply to get by in our society, and to meet the requirements of prospective employers? After all, is it not a central function of education to prepare children for adult life and the 'world of work' – to enable them to make their contribution to the growth of our modern industrial and technological society? Might not an education that focuses on depth of intellectual thought and understanding be in danger of ignoring these basic practical needs of many pupils and society in general? And now, since it would no doubt be over-simple to assume that these aims are mutually exclusive, a further important question arises: in what ways, if any, is the development of these other qualities related to the development of thinking and understanding?

To make progress on any of these important questions one thing seems unavoidable: we must try to get clearer about what thinking and understanding *are*! Not, I hasten to add, in the sense of expecting to arrive at some neat definition – the notions involved are much too subtle and complex for that – but in the sense of grasping more adequately the extent of this complexity and characterizing some of its important aspects and their interrelationships. Only then can we be in a position to judge the contribution of thinking and understanding to other important facets of human development and competing suggestions regarding the aims of education. And subsequent upon our answers to these questions, we may then be able to formulate guidelines and criteria for both the teaching approaches necessary to foster their development in children and also suitably sophisticated and flexible mechanisms of monitoring and assessment. These will be some of the main themes of this book.

However, before pursuing them, there are some important preliminary points that need to be made. The first is that not all the aims popularly attributed to education should go unquestioned, either in terms of the degree of emphasis placed upon them or, indeed, their very interpretation. Every educational aim represents a value position, i.e. a view about the 'good life' and the 'good society', that itself stands in need of justification. It is encouraging one or other version of what is to be valued in life and in our social arrangements. And what constitutes the most worthwhile or fulfilling sorts of life to lead and the kind of society that will best allow these to flourish is a matter of considerable moral and political debate.

Take the previously mentioned claim that education should prepare for the world of work. It might be thought that this seems straightforward enough: everyone needs to be able to earn a living. But questions of interpretation and emphasis would be very important here. 'Work' in any society is always undertaken in a particular social/economic/political context. If we consider this context in the case of our own society it clearly could not be taken as self-evident that the values and attitudes of the 'market-place' are the ones that should pervade education or life in general.[2] Attempts to introduce such values into the caring professions and services have attracted large-scale criticism, and presumably few would see them as forming an appropriate basis for, say, family life and the realm of personal relationships as a whole. (They would also clearly be antithetical to long-standing educational notions of the pursuit of truth and beauty in their various forms for their own sake, or the intrinsic enrichment they give to the life of the mind.) We need to be able to earn a living but, for many, earning a living in our society is a means not an end. Nor, given that it is still true that the majority of the workforce is involved in repetitive and intellectually undemanding jobs, can the world of work properly set the goals of education in any very extensive way. A piece of recent research has shown that for 87 per cent of the workforce of one urban community the most demanding and skilful thing they did each day was to drive to work.[3] And all this, of course, takes no account of the significant number of long-term unemployed.

Clearly, preparation for the world of work as an educational aim needs to be carefully analysed for its different interpretations and each of these needs to be considered in terms of how it would relate to other, perhaps more central, educational aims connected to the full development of the individual person in a democratic society. Now it is largely beyond the scope of this book to address these wider matters systematically, but it is important to recognize that teaching and education cannot be dissociated from contentious issues relating ultimately to conceptions of the 'good life' and the 'good society'. We will unavoidably be drawn back into some of them during the course of our enquiries.

The second important point that needs to be addressed is the following: does not the Education Reform Act of 1988 make any questioning of the kind that I am inviting a purely academic exercise? While I intend to examine (in Part Four) some of the detailed implications of this Act, it is, I think, important to address immediately this particular issue concerning the role of the teacher and others responsible for curriculum decisions within the primary school.

The first important thing to recognize in this regard is that the framework that the Act provides is far broader and less specific than the version of the National Curriculum which finds its way into schools at any particular time. This is amply evidenced at the macro level by the fact that subsequent Secretaries of State for Education have been able to change quite significant aspects of the National Curriculum, such as the range and forms of assessment across the foundation subjects and the number and range of attainment targets in science, without having to change the legislation. Thus the helpfulness of the National Curriculum in its various aspects is not a given, but something which has yet to be developed and demonstrated. Then again, at the micro level it has to be interpreted by those who are implementing it in a way that is to the educational benefit of the children in their care. It has to be seen as something which must evolve in response to on-going professional judgement both within the classroom and, if necessary, in terms of its broader structure. Teachers as professionals have responsibilities for the future development of the National Curriculum at both these levels – though not of course exclusively.[4] For teachers and other interested parties to exercise such discretion responsibly it is clearly important that they have thought through for themselves the underlying issues that affect the quality of children's learning. They need a basis of understanding which is *independent of* the National Curriculum in order to be able to evaluate it and to avoid the excesses of dogma that accompany the ascent of a monolithic orthodoxy.[5]

Yet there is a further important aspect to this issue. It will be argued that as it stands at the moment, even for someone who feels highly committed to the National Curriculum, it is simply not possible to follow it in any straightforward way. This is not only because in teaching there are too many variables involved for *any* recipe to be successful in all situations, it is because the National Curriculum contains within itself many tensions and some outright contradictions. For example, this seems to be most strikingly true with regard to its aspiration for depth and quality of understanding at the same time as a considerable breadth of pre-specified knowledge. The achievement of both of these in anything other than token form is neither possible practically in terms of the time available, nor, it will be argued, logically in terms of the degree of openness that the development of real understanding requires. Thus the teacher committed to the National Curriculum is still placed in a position of having to decide priorities and emphases within its set requirements. Here again professional judgement will be required which will need to be informed by an understanding of the kinds of issues I have raised.

It is interesting to note here that this need will not be circumvented if – perhaps as a response to practical objections expressed by the profession – the breadth of content of the National Curriculum were to be significantly reduced. In such an event the problems of justifying what remained are likely to become that much more acute: why precisely *this* and not *that*? Also, if the scope of what is to be drawn on within the compulsory foundation subjects were to be narrowed, this would place renewed importance on the curriculum which lies outside them – the 'whole curriculum' of which the foundation subjects were originally intended to be only a part. In this scenario, then, the role of teacher discretion would achieve increased significance in providing an education that was balanced and best suited to her children.

Thus, notwithstanding the aspirations of some critics of the profession who have sought a 'teacher-proof' curriculum, and indeed possibly the hopes of some teachers themselves looking for a lightening of professional responsibilities, teachers have not yet been relegated to the role of mere operatives who mechanically follow instructions handed down to them. And as we will see, because teaching essentially involves a relationship between unique human beings there are many very good reasons why a significant degree of professional autonomy and discretion will always be necessary if they are to do the job properly.

Let me now move on to a somewhat different but equally important consideration. It is this: though as teachers we are usually involved in one stage or facet of the education of a group of children, in order to do our best by them we need to be able to place what we are doing in the context of their education as a whole. We need to be able to see how what we intend to do in one situation relates to experiences they have, or are likely to have, in other situations; we need to have a conception of what we are building upon and where we are going, i.e. the possibilities and the implications of the experiences we are giving to children in the present. In other words, we must develop as best we can an appreciation of the *organic wholeness* of a life as experienced by any individual – his sense of personal belonging and the belonging together of things – for that is precisely what each child has himself to come to appreciate at some point if his education is to contribute to his development as an integrated person living in a world of complex relationships.

Now it is important to recognize that this demand is not at all adequately accommodated by, say, looking back over what a child is supposed to have been previously taught or by knowing the content specified in different stages of the National Curriculum. This is because what constitutes organic life experience is not so much a matter of what is *taught* as what is *learnt*, and the quality of that learning. It was this latter point, perhaps, that was not sufficiently recognized by HMI when, over a period of some years, they called for greater continuity and coherence in project work in the primary school and assumed that this would be chiefly provided by increasing the degree of pre-specified structure in this area of work. This clearly seems to underplay the extent to which continuity and coherence *from the learner's point of view* are likely to depend upon opportunities for him or her to influence the content and manner of what is to be learnt.[6]

As educators, then, it simply is not sufficient to have an expertise in the teaching of a specialism (even if we are employed as a specialist teacher), we must at the least have as full an understanding as possible of the part that specialism may play in an organic life. It follows that as teachers, we ourselves have need of a way of thinking and understanding that can give us this larger perspective, for this – the forming of organic life experience – must be a case above all others where the whole is more than the simple summing of its parts. Amongst other things, I will hope to show during the course of this book the contribution that a philosophical perspective can make to this kind of thinking.

As a result of considerations such as those mentioned above, we seem to be placed in the following situation: Primary teaching remains essentially problematic. The requirements of the National Curriculum have always to be interpreted in the context of unique situations. They are in any case confused in significant respects and therefore incapable of being implemented in any straight-forward way. The detailed framework of the National Curri-culum is itself evolving and teachers as members of a key professional group can and should influence this. Further, and in any event, teachers are themselves moral agents responsible for what they do. The fact that they can be regarded as filling a social role should not be allowed to blind us to their ultimate personal responsibility for what they do under its auspices: they are accountable not just to the system, their 'line managers' etc., but to themselves and the children they teach.[7] Now these general aspects of the teaching situation raise many issues which the reflective practitioner cannot avoid. One of them will be: how best can I develop the thinking and understanding of the children in my care? And how does this aspect of their education relate to and contribute towards other legitimate educational aims? No authority, no institution – not even a democratically elected government – can simply *legislate* the truth on such issues; this has to be discerned by honest and open reflection. Here, then, is the key problem that we will be addressing in the rest of this book.

Finally, a point concerning the strategy I shall be adopting in the pursuit of this problem. The topic of thinking and under-standing is vast. It is one which has been of abiding interest to thinkers over a very long period of time, and has therefore generated a wealth of views and perspectives and a body of literature whose size is commensurate with this. Not only would it be a task way beyond the scope of this book to attempt to produce an adequate survey of this accumulation of material, it is not possible here to produce examples which could even claim to be representative of its range. However, in the spirit of my main intention these limitations may not be a disadvantage. By eschewing any ambition to 'cover the ground' it is hoped that some depth of thought may be achieved, and by focusing on a limited number of contrasting perspectives (basically two) it is hoped that some central issues will arise in a relatively clear-cut and manageable way which will invite, rather than overwhelm, readers' own thoughts on the matter so that they may begin to formulate their own positions.

Thus the approach taken is to look first, in a preliminary way, at some general issues relating to thinking and understanding and the curriculum (Chapters 2 and 3), and then to take up some of the central problems raised in the rest of the book. In Part Two we shall examine in detail some responses to these issues which derive from a viewpoint currently influential in educational thinking and which I have termed 'rationalist'. In Part Three we will subject this approach to criticisms deriving from a radically different perspective which seeks to reaffirm the importance of more intuitive aspects of thinking rooted in the development of children's direct awareness of their own individual existence and felt involvement with things. This latter perspective I have dubbed 'existentialist'. In Part Four I shall be concerned to relate the discussion to the general teaching context and institutional climate in which education operates in Britain today, particularly with regard to the requirements of the National Curriculum.

NOTES AND REFERENCES

1 For a recent reaffirmation of this approach to the teaching of language and literature, see, for example, the collection of essays *After Alice*, edited by M. Styles *et al.* (1992).

2 Some of the issues that arise in this respect are well illustrated in the debate between David Bridges and Charles Bailey concerning one of the seemingly more educationally friendly notions to be thrown up here – that of 'enterprise'. See Bridges (1992) and Bailey (1992). See also the discussion of the effects of the 'GNP code' on our outlook on education and values in Bottery (1990), pp. 26–32, and an interesting account of the corrosive effects and manipulative motives underlying the general application of managerial language to education in Frowe (1992).

3 See the research of Blackburn and Mann cited in Robins and Webster (1989), Ch. 6. This chapter as a whole provides an interesting commentary on the striking *lack* of skills that modern industry requires of its operatives.

4 This point was recognized by the National Curriculum Council, soon after the inception of the National Curriculum, in its publication *Curriculum Guidance One: A Framework for the Primary Curriculum* (1989). Para. 2.11 states that 'It is not appropriate, or desirable, in the Council's view, that all primary schools should follow the same pattern of curriculum organization. Schools vary in so many respects that such an

11

approach would be unlikely to succeed.' Then again under 'Key Issues' (para. 3.3i): 'More effective and coherent learning will take place throughout a school where there is . . . a shared understanding of, and commitment to, curricular goals' and '. . . real participation of all staff in curriculum policy making.' And finally, in its Conclusion we read: 'It is headteachers and teachers who will translate the National Curriculum into opportunities for learning and it is only through the imaginative application of professional skills that standards will rise.'

5 The importance of pursuing alternatives to commonly accepted truths, and the broader relevance of this to the welfare of a liberal democratic society as a whole, received its classic statement in J. S. Mill's attack on 'dead dogma' in *On Liberty*, Chs 2 and 3. Here Mill argued forcefully that accepted truths should be subject to on-going critical evaluation from alternative perspectives since if they cannot be defended from such criticism they should clearly be rejected, and if they can be so defended they are more securely established and their grounds are better understood. Either way, then, the result of such scrutiny aids the pursuit of truth, increases understanding of the issues and educates the participants through their active engagement in the debate.

6 See the references to this in the following DES reports: *Primary Education in England* (HMSO, 1978); *Education 5-9* (HMSO, 1982); *9-13 Middle Schools* (HMSO, 1983) and *The Curriculum from 5-16* (HMSO, 1985). A useful discussion of these can be found in Dadds (1988).

7 Some of the extended possibilities of this are explored by, for example, Henry Giroux who has called for teachers to act as 'transformative intellectuals'. A transformative intellectual is one who takes up the task of 'making the pedagogical more political and the political more pedagogical. . . . In the first instance, this means inserting education directly into the political sphere by arguing that schooling represents both a struggle for meaning and a struggle over power relations. . . . In the second instance, making the political more pedagogical means utilizing forms of pedagogy that treat students as political agents, problematizes knowledge, utilizes dialogue, and makes knowledge meaningful, critical and ultimately emancipatory.' In order to maintain this stance while having to work within 'the overall hegemonic role of the school and the society it supports' teachers will be required to work with any number of groups 'that advance emancipatory traditions and cultures within and without alternative public spheres' (Aronwitz and Giroux, 1986, Ch. 2). Presumably, as influences on children during some of their most formative years, primary teachers would have a particularly important part to play in this exercise. And extreme as its demands may sound to many (and despite some of the language in which it is couched), such a view does invite us to examine the extent to which we feel the teacher has a wider political role and in what this might consist.

CHAPTER 2
What's Involved in Developing Children's Thinking?

We will begin our reflection by asking some preliminary questions about the sorts of things we might ordinarily have in mind when we speak of developing children's thinking, and the ways it may relate to other aspects of a child's development. So, what counts as developing children's thinking? The following is a list of some possible candidates:

they know more than they did before;
they can think what to do in new situations;
they can discuss or explain something that they could not before;
they see something differently;
they feel differently about something;
they can work something out for themselves that they could not before;
they have some new thoughts, feelings, understanding, appreciation, awareness.

Perhaps the most obvious feature of each member of the list is that it seems to pick out something which is mental in character, i.e. it refers to something which in some sense affects or characterizes the mind of the child – the quality of his or her mental life. But it is important to note at this early point that to say this is not to deny that thought may also affect *behaviour*: an action can be more or less thoughtful and our undertaking a course of action will normally be related to what we think about the situation in which we are operating. It is important to recognize this, for it carries the implication that to develop children's thinking may also be to develop – at least potentially – the quality of their actions. Indeed, since actions (as against mere bodily movements such as twitches and reflex jerks) are purposive, i.e. they involve the expression of intentions on the part of an agent, one of the chief ways of improving their quality precisely will be to improve the thinking which is involved in them. Much has been written in philosophy about the relationship between thought and action – too much for us to go into here; but that action in some sense involves thought is a critical point for education, and we need to say just a little more about it here if we are to properly appreciate the implications of our investigations for teaching.

Thought and action

There are varying kinds of action, and several ways in which thought may be involved. While it may be obvious that thought is involved in certain clearly 'intellectual' kinds of actions, such as those involved in setting up a scientific experiment or playing chess, it is clearly no less involved in actions which are, for example, more physical such as playing tennis or football. While sheer physical capacity is of great importance in these activities, such capacity alone will not do. We still evaluate performance in these areas largely in terms of the degree of intelligence they exhibit *vis-à-vis* achieving the goals of the game. Skilful play remains largely a matter of *thoughtful* play. Thus we should not be surprised to hear trainers exhorting their charges to 'think about what they are doing', or to discuss matters of strategy with them. This is still true of sports where the emphasis is even more clearly placed upon sheer physical prowess or stamina, such as athletics.

In any action the agent has to have some conception of what he or she is doing, and how he or she is doing it, and this involves thought in some sense. It also means that the action can be assessed for its appropriateness to the situation and its success in achieving its goals. It is true, of course, that once learnt some actions, such as those involved in driving or dancing, can become automatic or mechanical – through practice or habit they may become relatively thoughtless. But there are three important things to notice about this. Firstly, to say that thought is involved in action is not to say that we are always consciously thinking about an action either before, or whilst, we perform it.[1] Secondly, nonetheless we must have some minimal awareness of what we are doing: if asked, we must be able to give some sort of account of it in terms of what we are doing and why.

To be unable to bring to mind any conception of what we believe ourselves to be doing (which may or may not, of course, accord with how others perceive our action) means that we are not 'doing' anything properly speaking, but merely caught up in certain bodily movements. Thirdly, even with actions that have become automatic, if we wish to improve them we usually need to pay attention to them again, i.e. start to think about what we are doing. It is this feature of actions that makes them educable, as against merely being altered through some sort of mindless shaping process such as reflex conditioning.

Acceptance of the claim that the quality of our thinking can affect the quality of our actions serves to underline, then, the general importance of the development of a child's thought for his or her education. This point is reinforced when we consider that there is yet a further respect in which the development of a person's thinking has been held to be central to their educational development – its relationship to the domain of feeling and attitudes.

Thought and feeling

In a way which somewhat parallels the claim that action properly so described involves thought, it has been claimed that emotions and attitudes also have thought at their heart.[2] For example, does not the ability to feel guilt assume that one has the concept of responsibility, which in turn assumes that one has some concept of causality? These are concepts that children take time to develop as part of their own thinking. Further, if we consider such emotions as anger, fear, jealousy, does not each of them involve some sort of cognitive appraisal of the world? Does not anger involve seeing one's situation as in some way frustrating, fear as seeing it in some way dangerous, jealousy as seeing it in some way unjust in that we perceive someone else as possessing something to which we feel entitled? It has been claimed that it is this 'thought' element in emotion that allows us to distinguish one emotion from another – thus envy is distinguished from jealousy in that the element of entitlement is missing in the former.

It also allows the possible further refinement of emotions and the possibility of educating them. For example, inappropriate fear of an object may evaporate when one learns that it is not actually harmful and inappropriate desire when one learns that it is. Of course there will always be counter-examples to this as in the case of phobias such as fear of spiders and addictions such as cigarette smoking. But there are two points to be noted here. Firstly, the fact that some appraisals are very resistant to change or that even when changed they are overridden by ingrained associations or overweening desire (thus our use of the language of 'phobias' and 'addictions') in no way detracts from the claim that feelings can be evaluated for their appropriateness and that appraisals involved in emotions can be improved – be better informed, more sensitive etc., and that this provides a basis for the education of the emotions. On this view developing sensitivity of emotional response will be largely a matter of helping children to achieve wider and more refined appraisals of situations, e.g. by putting themselves in another's shoes or noticing relatively subtle but significant features of a situation which they had previously overlooked. (The LION is in a cage! . . . The show-off is very lonely . . . The broken toy was unintentional . . . The big fast car pollutes the atmosphere more than the small one. . .)[3] Such considerations are perhaps pre-eminent in areas of education concerned to combat prejudices and stereotypes. Information and discussion which, say, deepens appraisals of the potential of individuals regardless of their gender, race or age, or develops an appreciation of the significance of different cultural traditions, may be vital in contributing to the formation of more appropriate emotions and attitudes in these important areas. The need for this can, of course, become quite acute in a democratic and multi-cultural society and identifying this kind of relationship between thought and feeling suggests a way forward.

Yet maybe this way of characterizing emotional development is too neat and puts too much stress on the intellectual? Perhaps it overlooks the way that, say, mood can colour our perceptions and appraisals and how in general our affective state forms a backdrop to, and motivates, the way we apprehend the world around us.[4] That there is a reciprocal relationship between thought and feeling – and the extent to which it is even helpful to separate the two – are issues whose clarification must await discussion in later chapters, but at this stage it must at least be clear that thought and feeling are intimately related and that how we develop children's thinking may therefore carry extensive consequences for the development of their emotions. With this in mind let us now return to the question of what counts as developing children's thinking.

Criteria of development of thinking: the issue of standards in education

To what extent does the list of qualities at the beginning of this chapter adequately characterize the development of thought? In addition to their saying something about the mental life of the child, they seem to share another general feature. They each represent an *achievement* of some kind: the child has acquired some new capacity, disposition, or awareness. But does each of the achievements of itself denote the development of thinking? For them to serve as criteria in this regard clearly much will depend upon how they are interpreted.

For example, to take the first item on the list, would simply knowing more facts than previously mean that a person's thought had developed? No doubt in some sense it would be conceded a considerable mental achievement to have learnt off the entire contents of a telephone directory, or for that matter the entire contents of the *Encyclopædia Britannica*. But, useful as either of these mental feats might be in certain circumstances, would this necessarily constitute the development of a person's thinking? Or does this latter require something more: perhaps that such facts as they have learnt come to be seen to exhibit some kind of pattern, or have enabled the person to grasp or apply something which was previously beyond them?

Similarly, do seeing something differently, feeling differently about something, or having new thoughts and feelings, themselves necessarily constitute the development of thought? Can any (new) way of seeing or feeling – any new thought – count as the development of thought, or could some be retrograde (e.g. as when a child who previously thought decimal points to be significant in numbers now came to think that they weren't)? That is to say, to count as development do not such changes have to meet certain criteria of quality, achieve some new, higher, *standard*? Indeed is not this idea of meeting relevant standards, in some sense, implicit in all claims concerning the development of thought? In which case what are these standards and where do they come from?

This idea of thought needing to match up to certain qualitative standards is perhaps what was really meant when thinking was earlier described as an achievement and perhaps suggests that to think well is something that has to be learnt, for are not standards matters of social convention, and therefore things one is born to rather than with? In which case are there not issues to be confronted concerning how these standards are to be selected? This may not seem a very pressing problem in some areas, such as mathematics, but in art, literature and morality problems are rarely far below the surface, and even in history, geography and science there are significant controversies concerning matters of interpretation and emphasis which would have implications for what would count as good thinking and would therefore influence approaches to teaching at primary level. Whether commerce with the Third World is to be thought of as trade or exploitation, the extent to which empathy enhances historical understanding, might be cases in point.

But, of course the issue of standards in education is much broader than this, and has been a focus for considerable public debate. For some years there has been much talk about the need to raise standards in the primary school, particularly with regard to the so-called 'basics' of reading, writing, maths, and more lately, science. Notwithstanding the fact that many of the views popularly expressed concerning the rise or decline of standards have yet to be adequately substantiated by research evidence, there are surely some very important prior questions to be asked about the nature of the standards in terms of which the debate is to be conducted.

Take an example which is currently very prominent in this regard – standards in reading. Is a good reader to be measured primarily in terms of ability to identify and pronounce words and provide standard definitions of them, or ability to engage with the meanings expressed through some kind of dialogue? In an interesting discussion of this point Victor Watson describes how he found many of the qualities of what he terms a 'responsible reader' to be present in a group of reception class 'pre-readers':

> Working with reception children in a school which has adopted an apprenticeship approach to reading has taught me that pre-readers discussing a story shared with a sympathetic adult show most of the characteristics of a responsible reader: they discuss the story; they listen to their partner; they show an extraordinary awareness of detail; they relate the story to their own lives; they consider alternative versions; they make moral judgements ('That is a *wicked* picture!' – said about an illustration of Gretel shoving the witch into the oven); and they make thoughtful decisions about whether they want to reread the story or choose another. Many of these 4- and 5-year-olds have become readers in this sense *before* they are readers in the more usual sense associated with interpreting print.[5]

The force of this sort of observation is not of course to suggest that 'interpreting print' is unimportant, but to get us to question any assumption that it alone should set the standard as to what counts as a good reader. For such an emphasis could well lead to incipiently good readers in the broader sense being 'discouraged, or silenced, or side-tracked'.[6]

Thus in the various areas in which children's thinking is to be developed there is a need to be alert to the nature of the standards being applied. Do they do justice to the qualities of understanding that we should be seeking to promote or do they represent an impoverished view? Presumably everyone who cares for education will support the endeavour to raise standards. But often the crucial first question to ask is this: Which standards should obtain and how should they be interpreted? Put this way, we are rapidly confronted with the underlying issue which is essentially at stake: the question of what is really to be valued in education and why. Clearly this is an issue which deserves careful analysis and reflection, but which is in serious danger of being conveniently obscured and short-circuited by protagonists in a debate who speak as if educational standards are themselves unproblematic and the only issue is how to raise them.

Finally, let us return once more to our initial list, for there are two other things that we might notice about its members. Firstly, one of them directly refers to observable behaviour, whilst the rest seem to refer to things that have happened primarily 'in the mind'. This perhaps alerts us to the possibility that thinking may be displayed in action rather than being present only as some sort of accompaniment to it. The skill with which a fisherman casts his line or a musician expresses the mood of a piece of music in the playing of her instrument might be examples of this – as may the way a child contributes to a discussion, reads a story or poem, applies paint or collage, performs in dance, drama, or P.E. etc. In this sense thinking need not be something that goes on only 'in the head' and the way we teach and assess such thinking – the nature of the standards referred to – would need to be matched accordingly.

Secondly, some members of the list seem to refer to active abilities (e.g. being able to work something out), while others (e.g. having some new awareness, or feeling and seeing differently) have a more passive quality: they seem to intimate ways in which we may be affected by things rather than active upon them. This all perhaps suggests that we should not assume that thinking is any *one* thing; maybe there are radically different kinds of thinking which are organized around quite distinctive sets of standards.

This is certainly a commonly held view in education. Thus teachers sometimes speak of developing thinking in different subject areas, or they identify different sets of 'thinking skills' such as 'research skills', 'communication skills', 'interpretative' and 'translational' skills. Indeed, it sometimes seems as if almost any situation which differs from another requires its own way of thinking. In order to understand what is involved in developing children's thinking, we need to sort out these issues, for the question of whether thinking is basically of one kind or of many will clearly affect the nature of our enterprise.

NOTES AND REFERENCES

1 This point can be followed up in more detail in Gilbert Ryle's book *The Concept of Mind* (1949). See, for example, his critique of what he calls the 'intellectualist doctrine' in Ch. 2, especially pp. 28–32.
2 See, for example, R.S. Peters, 'The education of the emotions' in Dearden *et al.* (1972).
3 This approach is developed in some depth and with special reference to the contribution of the arts by R.W. Hepburn, in 'The arts and

the education of feeling and emotion' in Dearden *et al.*, op. cit.

4 An interesting analysis of some of the possibilities here is provided by the Gestalt psychologist F. Kreuger in his 'The Essence of Feeling' (1928), translated by Magda Arnold and published in her collection *The Nature of Emotion* (1968). See also, a useful discussion of two differing views of the relation between emotion and the intellect in Dunlop (1984), Ch. 6. Here he contrasts R. S. Peters' emphasis on the cognitive with John Macmurray's view that: 'It is not that our feelings have a secondary and subordinate capacity for being rational or irrational. It is that reason is primarily an affair of emotion, and that the rationality of thought is the derivative and secondary one. . . . The emotional life is not simply a part or aspect of human life. . . . It is the core and essence of human life. The intellect arises out of it, is rooted in it, draws its nourishment and sustenance from it, and is the subordinate partner in the human economy. This is because the intellect is essentially instrumental.'

5 Watson (1992).

6 This point has been developed considerably further by some writers in the field. See, for example, Egan (1990), Ch. 2, where, in contrast to the notion of 'conventional literacy', he expounds a notion of 'comprehensive literacy', which derives from what has been termed 'the literacy hypothesis'. The 'literacy hypothesis' makes the claim that historically the advent of reading and writing, and subsequently the printed word, brought huge cultural implications such as to quite transform consciousness from how it was in the oral tradition. Literacy, through objectifying and giving a permanency to thought (since all knowledge and belief no longer had to be held in memory), made possible, and predisposed us towards, reflective abstract thought, scepticism, systematic conceptual organizations of ideas and data, a sense of objective history as against mythical stories supporting just our own culture, a sense of self separate from nature – indeed, the realm of modern rationality itself. Such qualities of consciousness Egan argues can, and should, be recapitulated by individuals (particularly he believes by children in the 8–15 age range) and constitute what he refers to as 'comprehensive literacy'. This notion clearly invites subscription to a set of standards vastly broader than those associated with the mechanical skills of decoding and encoding which he ascribes to 'conventional literacy'.

CHAPTER 3

How Should Children's Learning Be Structured?

The role of the teacher

The general point has been made that notwithstanding the introduction of the National Curriculum the teacher retains a responsibility for the organization of learning opportunities within her class and also a wider professional responsibility to the overall character of education. As a prelude to the question of structuring learning it will be helpful to amplify the nature of this responsibility a little further.

Basically it comes down to this: because the teacher is the person who has to mediate the curriculum in the specific contexts in which education occurs she must have a substantial interpretive and formative role to play. Not only is she generally in the best position to make informed judgements about the ability levels, concerns and interests of the children in her class, her own strengths and weaknesses, and the resources available, she is also the person who is most intimately involved in the interactive process of children's learning. She is the person who will have to respond to the myriad contingencies that arise on a minute-to-minute, day-to-day, week-by-week basis within her classroom. She is the person who has to make on-going decisions concerning how to create and sustain an environment within which *these particular children's learning* will be most likely to flourish. Who else can decide when something is or is not 'working' for a particular group of children at a particular time, at which point a different approach should be tried, and what approach is most likely to succeed?

In this sense, then, the curriculum always needs to be to some extent negotiated – always in part determined by the children's response to what the teacher presents them with. It therefore cannot be completely pre-specified in advance. Once it is properly acknowledged that it is what children learn rather than what the teacher 'teaches' that constitutes the child's education, even the most formal of teachers will have to be prepared to modify what they have planned in the light of children's responses to it. This is a clear instance of the important point made in Chapter 1 that teachers cannot be regarded as operatives mechanically following instructions.

There is, then, simply no escaping an area of professional decision-making that will clearly cover a wide range of aspects and will be at varying levels of generality. It will range from more immediate responses to, say, specific breaches of discipline and how to deal with a particular child's learning difficulty, to wider policies concerning, say, general rules of behaviour and interaction and the best way of communicating certain broad areas of curriculum content. These are the decisions that ultimately determine the curriculum a particular child will experience: decisions made on the ground by a particular practitioner or school staff. And these decisions will of course reflect the understanding and underlying educational values of those practitioners. It is thus essential for the practitioner to have thought these through: to have developed his or her own understanding out of which he or she can act intelligently in the face of changing circumstances. And this is not simply a matter of accepting proper professional responsibility for what one does, but takes account of another important facet of primary teaching. Given the level of personal involvement that working closely with perhaps thirty-plus young people demands, it is likely that a teacher must feel a substantial level of personal commitment to the policy she is following, and feel she personally understands it, for it to be undertaken with the best chance of success and personal satisfaction. Teaching in a primary school is simply not something that can be successfully undertaken 'at a distance'.

Given, then, this important element of a teacher's professional responsibility along with other more general aspects previously mentioned, how are we to make a start on the issue of structuring children's learning? How can judgements in this area be given some reasonably objective basis? It might be thought that one fairly obvious possibility would be to look at past or current practice for some initial guidance.

Past and current practice as a guide to structuring children's learning

Suppose we were to look at that relatively easily accessible, albeit crude, indicator of how a child's education is being managed: the timetable. It would probably be one of the first things that someone enquiring about how children's work in the classroom was organized would ask about. Taking factors of the kind outlined earlier into account, it is perhaps not surprising that despite the recent moves to introduce more uniformity into primary schools, if we were to look at the timetables for different classes in different schools we would notice some similarities and many differences. We would probably notice some differences in the names given to certain activities; we would certainly notice differences in terms of when they took place, and the amount of time devoted to them. For example one might find that something called 'creative writing' was timetabled to take place regularly on Wednesday mornings at eleven o'clock for one class, whilst in another, perhaps even in the same school, it does not appear at all. Similarly we may find that one class has 'project work' for three afternoons per week, whilst another has none. Even such commonly regarded fundamental subjects as maths and language will appear as such on some timetables and not others. Indeed, some classes largely operate without any firmly fixed timetable at all.

On the surface there appears to be considerable disparity. But, of course, this appearance can be deceptive and often covers an underlying curriculum which has many features common from one class to another. Thus it is no doubt true that language work and maths have always taken up a very significant part of the school week for every normal primary school class in the country, including those who do not have them labelled as such on their timetable, but, perhaps, do them during 'project work'. The same may well become increasingly true for science and the other 'foundation' subjects of the National Curriculum. Now whilst this apparent disparity is not merely a matter of different labels hiding common features (for what we call something may reflect how we think about it, and thus our approach to it – consider the way 'language' has been renamed 'English' in the National

Curriculum), there is undoubtedly a significant element of this. And then there is the other side of the coin: common labels can hide different features. The diversity of practice that might be going on under the label 'maths' could be very considerable, the emphasis ranging perhaps from doing carefully sequenced sets of computation exercises to engaging in investigations, working with concrete apparatus, or playing a mathematical board game or bingo.

This now leaves us with the problem: if the timetable is not necessarily a very adequate guide to the nature of the curriculum, what is? What are the basic considerations in terms of which children's learning should be structured and the curriculum can be properly understood?

One answer to this is that it is the *different ways of thinking* that should determine the underlying structure of the curriculum, for they represent the most fundamental means by which we organize experience. Knowledge, skills and techniques, may all be important, but these are all to some degree the product of thinking, it may be claimed. They also require thinking, i.e. have to be located in patterns of thinking, if they are to be understood and intelligently applied. So, are there fundamentally different ways of thinking which we employ to organize and make sense of our experience? And if there are, does it follow that it should be a central purpose of the curriculum to initiate children into each of them?

If we look back over the way that learning has traditionally been organized into separate subject areas, such as English, maths, science, history, geography, art etc., it would seem that there has been an underlying assumption that there are distinct and separate ways of thinking that children should master. And at an intuitive level this seems to make sense: surely, one might say, there are important differences to be recognized between doing science and art, or maths and history? It is not merely that in each of these activities the object of our attention is often different – maybe, in maths it's numbers or geometrical shapes, in science it's things in the physical world, in history it's how we lived in the past, in art it's beauty in its various forms – it's the way in which our attention is focused that differs. It has been said that in maths and science we look at things 'logically',

25

whereas in art and literature we look at them 'creatively' or 'imaginatively'. Another way in which this has been put is to say that maths and science are 'objective', while art and literature are 'subjective'.

Clearly, then, at an intuitive and commonsense level there are a number of assumptions in play which would incline us to think that traditional school subjects represent distinct kinds of thinking, and insofar as it is plausible to see such subjects as derivative of the distinct disciplines of thought researched in universities and other institutions of higher education, this view would seem to gain further credence. But, of course, everyday intuition and commonsense are strongly influenced by our own socialization, indeed they are largely the product of this. We, therefore, cannot be content to accept their deliverances unchallenged. And there are many questions to be asked in this particular case.

We might begin by noticing that even within some of these traditional subject compartments seemingly different kinds of thinking are taking place. Punctuation, composing or appreciating a poem, discussing the morality of a character in a novel or the underlying philosophy of its author, would seem to involve significantly different thinking capacities, yet might all feature in a series of 'English' lessons. Similarly, observing and attempting to explain certain land or rock formations, exploring the nature and development of human communities or trading arrangements, and analysing statistics on the economic growth of different world regions, while falling under the heading of 'geography' seem to encompass somewhat differing kinds of thought. If this is so, that is to say, if what typically goes on within a school subject can lack homogeneity in terms of the thinking and understanding being drawn upon, it is clear that we would need to look elsewhere than the structure of the traditional school curriculum in order to identify fundamentally different ways of thinking.

But perhaps this supposition that there are distinct ways of thinking is itself an illusion. Perhaps, as Dewey has been held to claim, there is only *one* proper way of thinking: the scientific or problem-solving approach.[1] The claim here is that, no matter what the subject-matter, thinking essentially proceeds in the same way. Put very schematically, it goes something like this. Firstly there arises a sense of puzzlement in the context of something we are doing. We next try to formulate this into an identifiable problem. This is followed by an attempt to generate hypotheses which would solve the problem and thus remove our original puzzlement. And finally we set out to test these hypotheses to see which, if any, works. If we find that one of our hypotheses does work, then thinking has been successful to that degree, concrete progress has been made and we can move on to deal with further puzzlements. If none of our hypotheses work, then we attempt to generate further ones or reformulate the problem.

Now, it seems to me, that much of our thinking is something like Dewey's description, and this is true whether it be in the area of maths, science, history, or art. But it is far from clear that this account does not raise as many problems as it answers. Consider the following important questions:

(1) This description may apply to much of our thinking, but does it apply to *all* of it? Is all valuable thinking a matter of problem solving? What of contemplation, ruminating, daydreaming, revelation, reverie, wonderment, thanksgiving and celebration? And what of human *dilemmas* as against problems? The former are things which we may have to learn to live with rather than solve, and how best to live with them will not be accomplished by attempting to dissolve them through some problem-solving technique.

(2) Does not this description itself incorporate different kinds of thinking, e.g. the 'creative' thinking involved in generating hypotheses as against the 'deductive' thinking involved in testing them?

(3) Despite the ability to describe it in common terms, are the thinking processes involved the same across subject areas? For example, is the capacity to generate hypotheses and see if they work the same in maths, as in science, as in interpersonal relations, or morality? Is mathematical creativity and critical acumen basically the same as when we speak of these things in the field of literature, say?

If we are to make honest progress on the issue of how to develop children's thinking we must try to give more careful answers to such questions than they often receive in much of the current public discussion concerning the nature of the primary school curriculum – including the merits or otherwise of the National Curriculum and how schools should respond to it. For example, we cannot simply assume that the Foundation Subjects represent the best way of packaging knowledge and understanding for assimilation by children; this must depend upon whatever logic there is to learning and understanding and the structure of knowledge itself. At its inception Kenneth Baker claimed that the subjects of the National Curriculum simply 'choose themselves',[2] but what is, say, Technology as a separate subject? What gives it its integrity and how is it to be distinguished from Science? And what of the many important areas of human experience and understanding that are not obviously represented as a Foundation Subject such as moral understanding, drama, or philosophy? In order to undertake the task of interpreting the National Curriculum in the way that is educationally best for the children we are teaching, such questions cannot be ducked. It is now time to turn to what I have dubbed the 'rationalist' perspective on developing children's thinking for some more systematic guidance on these important issues.

NOTES AND REFERENCES

1 Dewey (1933).
2 In an interview given on *The Education Programme*, broadcast by the BBC in April 1987.

Part Two
Some Answers: Rationalism and Thinking

CHAPTER 4
The Rationalist View of Thinking

He who will not reason, is a bigot; he who cannot is a fool; and he who dares not is a slave. Sir William Drummond (1585–1649)

Clearly, to grasp the perspective that rationalism has to offer with regard to the kind of curriculum that will best develop a child's capacity to think and understand, and how this relates to his or her general education and development, we need to get clearer as to what rationality itself means. Presumably it is a way of thinking that values the seeking and giving of reasons, but what, precisely, does this involve, and what are its effects on thinking and the kind of understanding of the world that results? I will try to provide some clarification of these issues first by drawing upon the work of some recent writers in the field, and then by exploring the underlying ideas that emerge in more detail.

Some characterizations of rationality

In their *Introduction to Philosophy of Education* Barrow and Woods characterize rationality in the following terms:

> It was Aristotle who first defined man as a rational animal, and he meant by this that man was to be distinguished from other animals in that he had the ability to think, calculate or reason.

> Man differs from other animals in that he is able to act purposively, to plan, to choose ends and adopt means, and in that he is able to control his environment rather than simply respond to it. He is able to memorize, to imagine, to foresee, to predict, to hypothesize. To use the imprecise term which in common language includes all such activities, man has the capacity to think . . .

> Clearly, when people talk of aiming to promote rationality or to make people rational, they mean they want them to think well.

> . . . a rational man is, by definition, one who approaches matters

with a concern and an ability to assess them by means of relevant reasoning . . .[1]

This characterization is useful in that it makes quite explicit two important features of the claims that are made on behalf of rationality and its underlying nature. First, it is clear that there is a tendency to equate rationality with *good* thinking, or indeed even with the 'capacity to think' itself. Second, it is clear that rationality is not entirely neutral in its stance towards things: it has its own inherent purpose, viz., to *evaluate* them. Rational thinking, therefore, attempts to subject things to some kind of scrutiny and control. This has an important, but often unrecognized consequence: since 'to evaluate' is precisely to judge the fitness or quality of something in terms of some further more general goal or standard, rationality ultimately sees things from a perspective which subordinates them to something other than what they are in themselves. Some of the more serious implications of this are explored in later chapters, but the manner in which it is achieved is made plain in the following quotation from R. S. Peters in *Reason and Passion*:

> The most obvious and all pervading feature of reason is surely the transcendence of the this, the here and the now. . . . Explanation, planning, justification, all share in common this obvious characteristic. They connect what is, what is done and what is to be done with the past and the future by means of *generalizations and rules*.[2]

Reason works by standing back from things, disengaging thought from the immediacy of what is present in the here and now so that it sees things in terms of their location in some more general explanatory or justificatory framework. This framework itself consists of sets of rules for classifying things and connecting the classes of things so produced. Rationality, then, produces for itself a certain kind of reality whose structure is determined by its classificatory rules. Peters goes on to point out that these rules have to be public, i.e. agreed and shared, so that anyone who knows them can check that they have been properly applied in a particular situation. It is the presence of such public tests of correctness that can 'guarantee objectivity and the escape from arbitrariness'; and it is for this reason that he regards science as 'the supreme example of reason in action', and the physical sciences as 'perhaps the finest product that yet exists of the sustained and controlled imagination of the human race'.[3] It validates its claims through appeals to universal laws that, in principle, anyone can test.

Before bringing the focus a little more directly upon educational concerns, it would, I think, be helpful to refer to one more writer to flesh out further some of the general features of the operation of rationality, and its relationship to 'good' thinking. David Pole, in a paper called 'The concept of reason', writes: 'Reason is the sole route to truth, or the only non-arbitrary route.'[4]

As with the previous writers, there is the claim that all good ('non-arbitrary') thought is subsumed under the heading of rationality, and again, this latter is characterized by Pole through its appeal to rules and standards. It is these that are seen as both relating thought to reality (e.g. as in judging that *that* is a dog), and relating one thought or aspect of reality to another, as in the making of statements such as 'The dog is in the doorway' or 'Dogs and cats are both domestic pets'. Thus the fundamental units of thought are *concepts*, i.e. categories in terms of which we classify things in accordance with features they are considered to have in common, and of which such particular things therefore come to be regarded as *instances*. But this, of course, is not the end of the story: these concepts themselves belong to further conceptual schemes or theories by being subsumed under other, more general concepts than themselves (such as 'dogs' and 'cats' both being 'pets' or 'living organisms', etc.) with all the additional elements of significance that this brings with it. In this way, rational thinking performs the task of bringing the 'brute data' that we receive through the senses to order, organizing it by means of a net of interrelated concepts through which everything in thought is given a place, *and therefore a meaning*.

Thus central to the operation of rationality is the making of judgements. Good thinking is based on seeing how things in experience measure up to the agreed criteria or standards relevant to deciding membership of the various categories in which they might be placed. It is a matter of judging when something is an instance of a more general category and of judging the relationships between different categories.

So far this has all been couched in rather abstract terms. Let me now give an example to illustrate these claims. Imagine entering a strange room for the first time. The curtains are drawn and your eyes take time to adjust to the lack of light. Slowly you become aware of certain barely discernible objects in the dimness. Now what they *are* in that experience, i.e. what one understands them to be, will depend upon what categories you judge each of them to belong to. That long dark object over there, is it a bed or a sofa? Is that a pillow lying at one end or perhaps a cushion, and are those the ruffled sheets of an unmade bed or something else altogether? Clearly, one is here trying to define different aspects of the object to see if they match the requirements of one of the categories one has in mind. Your judgement on this will both define the reality of the object, and also, perhaps, the nature of the room you have strayed into: bedroom or sitting room. In turn, this judgement itself will set up a whole range of expectations concerning the other things in the room and will influence the way you interpret (i.e. *classify*) some of the other dim shapes you can just pick out. For example, the large dark shadow in the alcove opposite might on the one hand be perceived as a wardrobe, or on the other as a bookcase. The point is, what the thing *is* is decided by the category it is placed in: it's 'one of those'. Its significance, its value, indeed its very nature, is determined by this classification. This might be powerfully experienced if, in the context of the above example, while feeling our way around the edge of the darkened room we were to stumble upon a light switch and with some relief were able to clearly identify the objects as falling into the familiar pattern of, say, bed, wardrobe, curtains. Their nature is thus settled.

So, at its most fundamental level rational thought operates through seeing things as instances of categories. It makes experience manageable by organizing it in accordance with a complex set of publicly shared definitions (i.e. criteria, or standards). And these definitions determine what the thing is, if and how it is related to other things, and its place in the general scheme of things – that is to say, its meaning. Thus a child cannot see something *as* a tree, a triangle, or a tragedy until she has learnt what counts as being these things, i.e. the criteria by which they are distinguished. It seems to follow, then, that the categories –

concepts – which a child can apply in experience will be fundamental in determining the kinds of experience she will be capable
of having. They will determine what she can see, what she can
feel, and what she can understand. That is to say the very quality
of her experiences.[5]

Now for the most part, this categorizing is totally implicit in
experience, as in our unreflective use of concepts in our everyday
going about our business, but sometimes this is all done very
explicitly, as in attempts at scientific explanation. For example,
the theory of evolution brings otherwise disparate phenomena
such as adaption, competition, and gene mutation into relationship, and in so doing gives them added significance. Indeed, each
of these elements is itself a relationship between less abstract
elements, 'adaption', say, claiming a relationship between the
physical or behavioural constitution of the organism and its
habitat. And so on down a hierarchy of ever more primitive
elements in the explanation. (For the rationalist, something of a
parallel kind would be at the kernel of any sort of explaining: how
else can connections between things be made than through linking
them into conceptual schemes?)

Similarly, things change their meaning (and their value) as we
reclassify them for new purposes. Again this is happening all the
time in ways of which we are often not consciously aware, as when
some subtle shift in our view of another person occurs over a
period of time. But this, of course, might be far more explicit in
the case of, say, a detective in the process of investigating a crime.
Here as the investigation develops and new evidence comes to
light, things and people may become radically reclassified and
their significance radically altered. Thus an occurrence that
originally seemed trivial may take on a new cogency, someone
initially thought of as honest now seems dishonest, a sound alibi
now appears fatally flawed etc.

The central point is that throughout this process the meaning
and value of the things under consideration depend on two things:
first, the categories in which they are placed; second – and
this is very important – *the purposes or motives that underlie our
categorizing activity*. Arguably, categories are not simply present –
ready-made and manifest – in the physical world; they are
applied to the world by conscious beings in the course of their

interaction with it. But such interaction always has a purpose, or complex of purposes, which will heavily condition the kinds of categories that will be applied in particular experiences. Thus differing purposes may yield very differing views of the same phenomenon: what a child sees as a tatty toy an antiquarian may see as a treasure (and vice versa!). In this way our perception of things is never 'neutral'.[6]

Some broad considerations raised for teaching

This preliminary account of the operation of rationality in thinking leads to a number of general points with regard to the development of children's thinking. The first is that it makes absolutely clear what the central task of the teacher must be at whatever level: to help children to acquire an increasingly refined system of categories for classifying things. If things only have their meaning and value according to the categories in which we place them, then clearly it is crucial that children learn the shared public rules and standards involved in doing this. This will be central to their very ability to experience things, and to the quality of that experience.

This leads to a further point. Insofar as these standards are matters of social convention, which, for example, may differ in some regards from culture to culture, and since they are clearly very large in number (just consider all the things and relationships an adult in our society can conceive of), it would appear that they will need to be deliberately taught rather than picked up by chance. This requirement seems to receive further support from the observation that a great many public concepts are not manifest on the surface of the world simply to be discovered by the use of the senses. For example, while a child may be able to see, hear, touch etc., and learn shared labels for such purely physical properties as colours, sounds and textures, and maybe also physical things such as plants and animals, there are many categories whose defining attributes cannot be perceived through the senses in this way. One cannot in the same way simply 'see' such things as 'uncle', 'freedom', 'multiplication', 'atom', or even 'school'. Acquiring such concepts is more than – or not at all – a matter of observing physical properties, but a matter of grasping various abstract relations and social or theoretical purposes which will need to be explained by someone who already understands them.

Arguments such as these, then, seem to support the extensive (but not exclusive) use of instruction to demonstrate to children the relevant rules, standards and relationships; the provision of clear definitions and illustrative examples, followed by practice in applying what they have learnt to new experiences arranged by the teacher.[7] Further, and arising from the observation that rational thinking is not neutral, it will involve getting children to understand the purpose which the use of certain sets of categories serves. Thus developing their thinking in the area of, say, science will not be adequately described in terms of them coming to know certain classificatory rules and standards, but will need to include some grasp of the nature of the enterprise of science: its motive to provide causal explanations of phenomena. Some, at least tacit, understanding of this would seem to be necessary if scientific concepts are to be intelligently applied in experience.

Now it seems to me that both 'content'-based and 'process'-based views of primary science are in danger of paying too little heed to this. Of themselves, neither factual knowledge nor acquiring so-called 'skills' of observation, hypothesizing and testing contribute much to scientific understanding unless they are taught in a way that conveys the character of the underlying achievements being sought: the quality of scientific explanation and its purpose. For example, the appropriateness and accuracy of an observation will clearly be dependent upon an understanding of the sort of thing you are looking for and why. Similarly, the usefulness of an hypothesis will depend upon an understanding of the sorts of questions to ask in a particular context. That is to say, there is a danger here of conjuring up the chimera of teaching a set of free-floating 'skills' when what is really required is *understanding* – through which skills are embedded in an apprehension both of what in general counts as and motivates a scientific enquiry and of the rationale of a particular investigation under way. Skills, conceived as specific abilities, remain 'blind' if not underpinned by such understanding of the contexts in which they are to be applied. In a parallel way the same can no doubt be said for other curriculum areas such as history and geography where 'knowledge' and 'skills' talk sometimes dominates debate about what should be taught.[8]

It is clear, then, that the demands for the development of rational thought go well beyond the mere rote learning of facts and mechanical thinking skills. There may be an emphasis on instruction in teaching, but it will be of a form intended to lead to a certain kind of understanding on the part of the pupil such that he or she is able to apply what they have learnt to their experience in a coherent and publicly accepted manner. But there are perhaps some important questions being begged by the account I have so far given. Questions largely to do with the place of individuality of thought and the possibilities of individual discovery, invention and creation in the development of thinking. Some exploration of these questions, and an examination of more developed and sophisticated rationalist perspectives in education which attempt to deal with them, will be taken up in the next chapter.

NOTES AND REFERENCES

1 Barrow and Woods (1990), Ch. 6.
2 R.S. Peters, 'Reason and passion', in Dearden *et al.* (1972).
3 Ibid.
4 D. Pole, 'The concept of reason', in Dearden *et al.*, op. cit.
5 For many, this sort of point has come to have the ring of truism about it and is perhaps now something of a commonplace, but the incredible power of publicly shared concepts to transform existence is brought into sharp focus when we recall the following episode taken from Helen Keller's life, recounted by Mickie Davidson in *Helen Keller's Teacher*:

   Helen was blind and deaf. Soon the few words she had learnt before her illness withered on her tongue, and soon she was mute too. Her body continued to grow, but her mind was cut off in the dark silence. She seemed more like a phantom than a child – a phantom wandering through a world she could no longer understand. . . . Then came Annie.

   One morning Annie led Helen down to the old well house that stood at the foot of the garden. Helen loved to play in its cool dampness, so now she scurried cheerfully inside. Annie took a deep breath and followed. She began to bang the pump handle up and down, and soon a stream of water poured from its lip. She grabbed Helen's hand and stuck it under the icy flow, and in the same instant began to spell W-A-T-E-R into the wet palm.

   Helen went rigid and pulled wildly towards freedom. But Annie held on.

W-A-T-E-R . . . W-A-T-E-R . . . W-A-T-E-R – she drummed the word faster and faster into Helen's hand.

Suddenly Helen stopped struggling. Or breathing. Or doing anything except concentrating on the shapes in her palm. W-A-T-E-R. She felt the word burn down through her hand and into her brain. W-A-T-E-R . . . a light flooded across her face.

W-A-T . . . she began to spell the word back to Annie. And with each movement of her own fingers, the namelessness retreated. She understood! These movements stood for the cold liquid that was pouring over her hand! They always stood for that, and nothing else! She understood! . . . The little girl who'd been locked away in dark silence would never be quite so lonely again. She would never see the world outside. She would never hear it. But she was learning to communicate.

She could talk with her fingers and listen with her palm.

6   The general point concerning the way human purposes condition our whole categorial apparatus is discussed from an interesting perspective by Ernst Cassirer (1946) in *Language and Myth*, Ch. 3. Here he argues that the classical theory of abstractionism which supposes that concepts are formed through comparison and the abstraction of shared properties may characterize the formation of an upper stratum of concepts produced through the activity of intellectual discursive thought, but this itself presupposes that there are pre-given properties in experience to be so denoted. Thus there is a need to postulate a lower stratum of what he terms 'primordial linguistic concepts' which he believes are the product of a process of mythico-linguistic 'naming'. Here, far from ideation being the result of a reflective comparison of attributes, the attributes themselves are posited by a process of extreme condensation in which they are first heightened and thus to some extent stabilized in experience as 'momentary gods' which arise without discursive reference to anything beyond themselves. They are experiences in which the subject is totally absorbed in the here and now of the phenomenon itself. The empirical claims being made here about the character and contribution of mythical thinking (interesting and important as I think they are) are not for us at present so much the issue as the clear recognition that 'noticing . . . must precede mentally the function of denoting' and that the direction of our noticing will be conditioned by our purposes. Thus, on this view, both the concepts formed through intellectual discursive thought *and the particular properties that it works upon* – selects and brings into combination – are thoroughly conditioned by human purposes and practices. As Cassirer himself puts it:

> the recognition of function precedes that of Being. The aspects of Being are distinguished and co-ordinated according to a measure supplied by action — hence they are guided, not by any 'objective' similarity among things, but by

39

their appearance through the medium of practice, which relates them within a purposive nexus. (p. 39)

7 It is important to note that the view is also clearly compatible to some extent with the use of what Dearden (1967) has termed 'guided discovery' in which the teacher constructs a learning situation - perhaps by setting a problem in a certain context - in which the child arrives at some knowledge new to her for herself. But given the sheer volume of concepts to be learnt and the abstract character of many of them previously noted, together with the likely practical constraints, this approach could only be advocated on a limited scale by the rationalist. However, as will be seen in subsequent chapters, if the scale of this approach must necessarily be limited, its contribution might be of the greatest importance to fostering some of the qualities of thinking which rationalism requires.

8 Some of the confusions and educationally unsound motives that inform much loose talk of 'skills' in education are explored in Barrow (1987) and Smith (1987). See also F. Smith (1992), Chs 2, 6, 7, for a sustained attack on the notion of separate, generalizable 'thinking skills' - though I find his general account confused in some places. The issue will also be revisited when we consider the views of Paul Hirst in Chapter 6.

CHAPTER 5

Rationality and the Individual

In Chapter 4 I outlined the way in which rational thinking operates by the application of publicly shared systems of classification to experience, i.e. conceptual schemes, which themselves express certain purposes or motives with regard to experience. We noted that the use of such schemes involves the application of shared rules and standards in accordance with which things are placed in their proper categories, and that this placement defines the thing both in terms of its meaning and its value. We then raised some questions concerning the place of individuality in the development of thinking in the context of a view which places so much emphasis on social convention in the structuring of thought. By way of developing these important issues, and the way in which the rationalist view might deal with them, I would now like to refer to some central ideas developed by some recent thinkers in the tradition. In considering these ideas, we will see how rationalism modulates the idea of human individuality within a framework of social conventions such that the very idea of an individual human mind comes to be seen as parasitic upon them. The first of these views develops this theme by looking at the relationship between the possibility of developing a person's thinking, i.e. his or her mind, and his or her culture.

Michael Oakeshott: Individual and culture[1]

Michael Oakeshott's view of the relationship between the development of the human mind and culture is nicely summed up in the following claim: 'Human being has a history, but no "nature".' Oakeshott strongly believes that we are misled if we think of the development of an individual human being as akin to a process of growth in which some innate or settled nature unfolds – as, say, in the way that the mature oak tree is predetermined by the genetic endowment of the acorn. He wishes

41

to stress the point that human development is basically a matter of an on-going transaction between an individual and the human world, and that our individual humanness is therefore not simply prefigured, but the product of a history of such transactions from birth. Now the important thing about this is how he goes on to characterize the human world. He makes the point that the human world is not essentially a world of mere physical things, but of *intelligibles*, i.e. understandings, significances, beliefs, ideas, etc. Thus everything in a human world from everyday things such as chairs and postboxes, to institutions such as marriage and the family, or schools, colleges, and the Houses of Parliament, are what they are according to the meaning they have within a social form of life. It is this shared way of living together that forms the context and the material for the growth of any individual, determining both what is possible and what is valuable.

So of what, fundamentally, is this shared way of living composed? And how precisely does it enter into and shape the development of the individual? Oakeshott suggests that at base our human world is made possible by a wide range of *shared procedures* through which meanings and significances are given and communicated. Over the period of our history we have developed, and continue to develop, sets of social rules, conventions and standards for discriminating and evaluating things. These shared procedures permeate and give sense to all aspects of our life, governing both thought and behaviour. They constitute our culture in its broadest and deepest sense and structure aspects of our lives as various as, say, buying some breakfast cereal to writing a will or offering up a prayer. It should be stressed at once here that this view of culture does not see it as static, but rather, to use Oakeshott's own analogy, as an on-going 'conversation'. In this conversation, which began with the dawn of human awareness, the languages of feelings, sentiments, desires, recognitions, moral and religious beliefs, intellectual and practical enterprises etc. interplay, constantly creating the parameters and possibilities for human being. It is only through engaging in this conversation, entering the interplay of these various languages, that 'self-disclosure' and 'self-enactment' of the individual can occur. We find out who we are, and express ourselves, by participating in the sets of shared procedures (or 'languages') that are our culture. All talk of human or individual potential presupposes this.

It can be seen, then, that culture, in Oakeshott's sense, is not a set of rigid formulae or recipes for thought and behaviour. In a language one can say many things, though not *anything* (e.g. we cannot say with literal meaning that 'justice is pink'). Rather, for Oakeshott, culture is living, and represents invitations for engagement in the conversation of humankind. Through such engagement culture is continuously invented and added to. But where does this leave the individual? For we are all born *into* a culture, but not *with* a culture. Oakeshott is uncompromising on this: '. . . nobody is born a human being'. If being human consists precisely in participating in sets of historically developed procedures, this is something that must be *learnt*, for 'to be without this understanding is to be not human, but a stranger to the human condition' (p. 21).

Studies of so-called 'wolf-boys' – boys raised by wolves from birth and who, when found, exhibited the behavioural characteristics of their surrogate parents – might be taken to amply demonstrate the truth of this claim.[2] Before we can properly be said to have entered the human condition, we need to have acquired the basic social rules, conventions, standards, i.e. procedures, that enable us to participate in and contribute to culture. Thus education must be seen as an initiation into this inheritance of understanding and belief.

This is not, however, quite the end of the story, for at this point Oakeshott adds an important caveat. Culture – these procedures, this conversation – is not to be equated with the talk and bustle of the everyday world whose current engagements and occupations are directed at more immediate results. Here, in the hustle of consumerism, sensationalism and passing fashion, in the blandness of mediocrity and preoccupation with immediate practical gain, Oakeshott believes that the true conversation has largely been forgotten, abridged, and corrupted. Culture proper, our 'civilized inheritance', is largely unfamiliar to both the child and everyday life. Thus schools should be, as they were originally, monastic in character, places set somewhat apart from the everyday world so that serious and systematic study can go on undisturbed, and where 'excellences may be heard because the din of worldly laxities and partialities is silenced or abated'.

This concern for true culture to be 'heard' by the child leads Oakeshott to reject both child-centred approaches to education and the notion that the basic aim of education is socialization (i.e. it should be dominated by what is considered to be 'socially relevant'). He fears that the former, with its emphasis on children's interests, will distort the enterprise of enabling engagement with what is to them, by definition, an unfamiliar inheritance of human achievement. (If it were familiar, presumably children would not need to go to school.) He fears that the latter with its attempt to make people 'current' – attuned to the changing needs of a largely unauthentic society which has forgotten its 'civilized inheritance' – would be to shirk the central duty of a real education.

Now it seems to me that this view draws a number of important aspects of education to our attention which do more than simply act as a timely deterrent to any tendencies we may have towards either rampant individualism, or elevating the norms and immediate needs of modern society as a central goal of education. It is of course hardly *de rigueur* to suggest that schools maintain a certain aloofness from the everyday life of 'the community', the demands of 'the customer', the 'needs of industry', etc., but perhaps there is an important issue at stake here? While there may be many good reasons why schools should not become *isolated* from society, may it not be of the highest importance for them to retain certain *distinctive purposes* which should not be reduced to whatever the current, perhaps most vocal, demands of that society happen to be? If the continuity provided by public traditions of thought give us a characteristically human world with its sense of security and purpose necessary for sustained engagement – if these traditions represent what is at the kernel of humanness in its fullest sense – they should not, and indeed cannot, be easily subverted or overturned. Rather they deserve a certain reverence which should be reflected in education.

This, in turn, serves to extend, I think, a point touched upon towards the end of the previous chapter about the need for content and skills to be embedded in a context of deeper understanding. When certain aspects of a subject are identified as central teaching objectives, comprehensively set out in a detailed and systematic manner, there may be a tendency for them to be taught rather clinically in an effort to cover the ground in the most efficient way. Oakeshott's view invites us to see them in an altogether different light: not just as curriculum subjects consisting of various components of facts, theories, concepts and skills – so many commodities to be 'delivered' – but as holistic traditions which embody that which is of enduring value and into which it is the sacred task of the teacher to initiate pupils. They are not simply to be made 'fun' or 'interesting' or 'relevant' (indeed, on this view they are the *standard* of what should count as relevant), but to be conveyed as *living traditions* with their own ethos, outlook and sense of illumination. Teaching must reflect this by re-embedding the components that may have been analysed out for planning and monitoring purposes in a developing sense of the tradition as a whole – presumably by reference to the great themes, moments, and figures which comprise it, and by conveying something of the fascinations, enthusiasms, nuances, moods which lend it its living character and which it contributes to the greater 'conversation' of which Oakeshott speaks.

In short, then, the overriding aim should be not merely for the various areas of the curriculum to be 'encountered' or 'delivered', but to be *lived*. As well as providing tremendous scope for the imagination of teachers, such an approach, of course, raises serious questions about how to provide a suitable curriculum framework, classroom organization and teaching ethos at the primary level. But it is also strongly suggestive of two aspects of the way forward. The first is that, given the character of what is to be conveyed, it would seem to speak in favour of some form of apprenticeship approach to children's learning. The second is that it could be taken as re-asserting the value of a perhaps currently oft-neglected but powerful source of motivation in education: *emulation* (in contrast to, but not necessarily in conflict with, competition, intrinsic interest, immediate relevance). These two aspects are clearly intertwined and I should like to say just a little more about them here.

It would seem that crucial to developing a sense of the life of a tradition is to work alongside someone who shares in that life. Someone with significant knowledge, insight and 'feel' for the area concerned and who exhibits this in their manner of going about things. While this does not necessarily support specialist teachers in primary schools it probably does require teachers with *specialisms*, i.e. strong abiding personal interests. Such role models can convey in a concrete and often incidental way the outlook and qualities of the traditions they have become engaged with – for to some extent here we are talking about ways of life, or important constituents thereof. For this to happen, though, children themselves would need to begin to engage in the *problems* and not simply the solutions in an area and to be able to discuss their ideas both freely and under the guidance of those with relatively greater insight and feel, who could draw judiciously on their own knowledge and experience in a way that integrates the thoughts of their pupils with the tradition.

In the process of doing this it would, in addition, be important to begin to establish a sense of *history*, i.e. that ideas have evolved, that certain basic themes have been of enduring importance and that 'real' people have contributed to their development, bringing to bear concerns that are both perhaps sometimes unique to individuals, but also reflecting their personal circumstances and broader social/intellectual context. Such an initiation might begin to help children get their own feel for the underlying sense and direction of the aspects of culture with which they are engaging by, as it were, 'listening in' to previous parts of the 'conversation', and to gain some appreciation of their impact on living a human life.

In the above ways, then, I believe that Oakeshott's brand of 'conservative rationalism' has important insights to offer us in primary education. But it also provokes some significant anxieties in relation to the question about individuality in thinking from which this chapter took its start.

Clearly, on this view individuality and creativity can come into play only on the back of the acquisition of culture, and in the form of relatively minor modifications to it which its established procedures permit. Indeed, on this account it would seem that individuality need for the most part involve no modification of culture at all, but simply an adherence to certain alternatives as against others contained within that culture. Thus a person's individuality may largely consist in such things as his tastes in music and size in slippers which cumulatively mark him out as different to most others. And much of this may be determined by contingent facts of his own physiology, subcultural background and events and occurrences in which he has happened to have been involved, which in turn will to some degree have been conditioned by the cultural milieu in which he happens to find himself. Now the question arises: is the notion of individual that emerges here adequate to what we have in mind when, for example, we speak of 'valuing each child as an individual' or of wanting to develop each child's 'individual potential'?

While Oakeshott's account rightly reminds us that in large degree it is culture that provides whatever means are available for expressing oneself, and that therefore a concern to develop individual potential must largely be understood in terms of initiation into the traditions that constitute culture, an important question is raised. Why should we value any particular individual, portrayed as this rather arbitrary combination of possibilities, as against his or her culture as such? That is to say, is there not a danger of this view inclining us to see and value individuals basically as representatives of their culture – and perhaps as potentially significant contributors to it – rather than for themselves? With regard to the latter, the temptation to give a relatively specialized and accelerated education to child 'geniuses' might be a case in point. In a more general way the dangers of cultural stereotyping of individuals, or of subordinating the feelings and real aptitudes of individuals to what is currently culturally valued, can be very real – for even 'high culture' can have its fashions and paradigms that preclude other worthwhile possibilities.

What seems to be seriously underplayed in Oakeshott's account is the sense of the child as an individual centre of consciousness exhibiting personal agency – which is perhaps one of the most striking things about, for example, walking into an infant reception class! In emphasizing the sense in which the human condition is something to be achieved rather than innately present, Oakeshott gives education a heavy future orientation in which perhaps rather too little attention may be given to individuals as they are *now* as compared with what they may have the potential to become in cultural terms. Consideration of his view thus challenges us to confront a question too rarely addressed: *why, and in what senses, should we 'value the individual' in education?* I pose this question not to deny the significance of human individuality, but simply in order to make the point that if we are to do anything constructive about its development in the primary school we must sort out what we mean by it.

We are, then, back with the problem as to in what true individuality is taken to consist, and how we are to understand aspects of a person's life (if any) which are not obviously to be accounted for in the terms invited by Oakeshott. This is underlined by what is perhaps a serious problem concerning Oakeshott's implicit distinction between the public procedures which he stresses and the substantive ideas, beliefs, sentiments, behaviours etc. which they generate. That is to say, is Oakeshott having to assume a hard differentiation between the *form* and the *content* of a social way of life? If he does, can it be maintained? (For example, do not procedures themselves partly consist in substantive ideas and beliefs produced by prior procedures, and indeed, do procedures have the logical priority over ideas that Oakeshott seems to assume?) If he does not, i.e. if acquisition of culture involves the acquisition of a large number of detailed and substantive beliefs etc., would this not be so constraining as to rule out the possibility of anything that we would want to recognize as the expression of individuality, for now not only the form, but the detailed content of the 'conversations' in which human beings participate would be predetermined? Such considerations raise starkly the issue of just what independent thinking consists in, and its relationship to the social conventions which structure the *status quo*. To pursue this, we will need to give some consideration to certain aspects of the thinking of one of the most influential mainstream philosophers of this century: Ludwig Wittgenstein.

Wittgenstein: Rules, meaning, and freedom[3]

One of the contributions that Wittgenstein made to our understanding of issues in this area was to introduce an analogy between human activity and games. One form of human activity is that of understanding itself, and Wittgenstein began by trying to characterize the conditions under which we would be prepared to say of someone that he or she understood something, or had the concept of it.

Suppose we wished to teach a child the idea of a number series such as that formed by the three times table. Perhaps, amongst other things, we ask the child to colour in this series on a one hundred number square. Maybe at first she colours numbers in a relatively random manner, but with further guidance colours them as follows: 1,3,5,7,9,11,13, etc. Here the numbers have not been coloured in a simply random fashion, but have been coloured in a way that incorporates a systematic mistake: the child has 'counted on' according to the logic 1,2,3 – 3,4,5 – 5,6,7 etc. Clearly – and it would be important to recognize this – it's not that the child has *no* understanding at this point, rather that she has a *mis*understanding, which is a very significant step towards a proper understanding. Perhaps the teacher now explains this mistake and gets the pupil to colour in the first few correct numbers. Now should we at this point say that the child has understood this series of numbers? Wittgenstein would say no, to demonstrate this she must colour more of the series which she has not been shown directly how to do by the teacher. The point here, then, is that it is only when people show themselves able to *carry on independently* in new situations that we would be prepared to say that they have understood. Parallel examples could be drawn from the area of language such as the learning of punctuation, or the past tense ('I catched', 'I fighted'), or the acquisition of new vocabulary where a child uses a new word slightly inappropriately, its meaning being understood in one context only. The general point is that many mistakes are stages in the growth of understanding, and that this is considered to be achieved only as the child develops his or her own capacity to respond correctly in new situations.

But, now, in what precisely does such understanding consist? Is there some specific underlying feature that lies at the kernel of this capacity to carry on independently in new situations? The kinds of example we have been describing are taken to show us several important features concerning the general nature of understanding.

The first of these is that understanding cannot simply be

some private inner mental occurrence such as a sudden feeling or flash of insight. Clearly we could experience such a feeling but not really have understood. Someone's crying 'Aha!' or 'Yes, now I see!' cannot be taken to guarantee that they've got the right end of the stick. But if understanding is not to be equated with some private feeling, nor is it to be equated simply with public behaviour. Surely, it is not the actual behaviour of 'carrying on' itself that constitutes understanding, for, to take the number series example, we would not assume that understanding suddenly ceases the moment the pupil stops writing. Nor would she need to actually continue the series *ad nauseam* in order to understand how this would be done. Thus behaviour may exhibit understanding, but cannot be equated with it. So what is understanding itself? Wittgenstein suggests that the child's understanding simply consists in her *being able to follow a rule*. She has acquired the capacity to think in accordance with a guiding principle, by reference to which she is able to distinguish correct and incorrect ways of proceeding. Further, this capacity is not a quality which is *added* to thought, it *constitutes* thought itself. Thought (and understanding) *is* this capacity of linking things together and distinguishing them from other things not in some random or arbitrary way, but systematically, i.e. in accordance with a guiding rule.

Now it may at first blush seem that this notion of thinking and understanding as a matter of rule-following is somewhat unremarkable and almost too simple and innocent to warrant further attention. But a little reflection reveals some very significant implications which have wide-ranging ramifications. To begin with, it carries the following important corollary: thinking and understanding are essentially *public* in character. Whether a person is following a rule is not in principle a purely private or subjective matter, it is an essential part of the nature of a rule that all who know it are in a position to decide when it is being followed. Further, even if a person invents a new rule for himself, and does not tell others what it is, while it may be open to him to *change* the rule according to subjective whim, it is not purely a matter of subjective whim as to whether he is *following* the original rule. If he privately invents a rule, say, of behaviour for himself and then ends up doing something else, no matter what he, himself, might believe or wish, he simply is not following his own rule. Indeed, in some circumstances, if others were to infer from his previous behaviour what his 'secret' rule was, or he were to divulge it to them, they may on occasion make a better judgement as to whether he is following his own rule than he can.

The important point is, that to follow a rule is to have a standard of reference which is in a very significant sense *independent of oneself*, even if it were one's own invention. But there is a second point to be made. The vast majority of rules which are important in human life are not only public in principle, they are public in fact. The whole of social life, including language and the accumulated knowledge and understanding of a culture, is based on a structure of publicly shared conventions, i.e. rules. Without this we would not even be able to communicate with others, to convey or compare our experiences. Imagine the chaos of a world in which, like Lewis Carroll's Humpty Dumpty, each individual simply gave to words whatever meaning he or she wished them to have at the time: where the meaning of, say, a request to 'pass the salt' or the promise 'I do' was down to the free play of an inventive mind. Wittgenstein's account brings out the way in which thinking and understanding must have a strongly public and therefore *objective* character – shared rules enabling comparisons to be drawn and others to understand and check on what one says. It follows on this account that the promotion of understanding in an individual will precisely consist in acquiring more such shared rules for the structuring of their thought.

So far we have taken as our starting point a fairly simple case: the understanding of – or having a concept of – one particular thing. But what of the whole bodies of understanding we began to make reference to in the last paragraph? How are we to characterize, say, the disciplines of maths, science, history, etc., to which schools wish to introduce pupils (even if they are not necessarily taught as separate subjects, but through an inter-disciplinary approach)? It is at this point that Wittgenstein's analogy with games has been thought to be illuminating and will help to illustrate many of the points stated in more abstract form above. The point about games is that they are quite explicitly rule-structured activities, and therefore if we examine the way that they function we may gain insight into the way aspects of human life which are more tacitly rule-structured operate.

Suppose we were to witness the following incident. A number of men wearing shorts are running about on a field seemingly chasing a ball. The ball passes between two white posts with a bar across the top, and this is immediately followed by the sound of a whistle emanating from a figure dressed in black, whose shorts are a little longer and baggier than those of the other members of the group. He then raises his arm, whereupon a number of the men begin to embrace each other while others stand dejected or begin gesticulating at the black figure. Someone unfamiliar with the rules of this game may wonder what all the fuss is about. The events that he has witnessed can only take on their significance for him when he gets to know these rules. For example that the object is to get the ball between the posts, but not in any old fashion – there is to be no handling of the ball, nor deliberate obstruction of opponents, and the ball has to be kept within the white lines which mark the perimeter of what is called the 'pitch', etc. Such rules structure the activity, give it its purpose, and make it the activity that it is. They indicate which particular events are important. For example, one goal-keeper stamping to keep warm is not important while the other diving for the ball is. They determine how things are to be classified, e.g. as 'goal', 'foul', 'offside'; and how things are to be done, such as the taking of a free kick or a throw-in. Importantly, it follows from this that the rules will also determine the meaning of the terms and statements relating to the activity and how one would verify them. For example, the meaning and truth of the claim 'That's a goal!' is not a subjective matter, it will be determined by the relevant rules. And, of course, what is to count as important, as success, as true or false, will be different for other games. Goals are scored differently in Rugby football, and not at all in chess.

Now the claim is that much characteristically human activity, including the pursuit of truth and understanding, is structured by complex sets of rules in ways analogous to games. Thus to take the 'game' of natural science, it can be seen to be structured and given its identity by its distinctive body of rules. The rules determine what is to count as a scientific explanation: that it must ultimately be testable against observation through the senses. The rules determine what counts as a satisfactory scientific experiment, for example that there should be controls, that it should be repeatable. The rules determine what data are or are not significant (e.g. the scientist's subjective wishes and feelings are not relevant). The rules determine the manner in which scientific observations and conclusions should be written up, and so forth.

But as well as these rules of procedure, there are what one might term *rules of content*, i.e. the rules used to organize and classify the content of experience in shared ways, to which we have made previous reference. Thus as well as its distinctive procedures, science has its distinctive concepts, such as those of 'causality', 'energy', 'velocity' and webs of concepts, such as the theory of evolution, which give direction to the enterprise as a whole, or particular aspects of it, and thus delineate the terrain within which the scientist works. So to understand what a scientist is about requires an awareness of such rules, and to learn to do science is to learn how to apply them in one's own experience, i.e. to learn how to 'play the game'.

Similarly, just as there are different games to be played in the conventional sense of that word, so the search for truth and understanding in different areas, i.e. the different disciplines of thought, might be thought of as comprising different games: different sets of rules constitute different forms of rationality giving rise to different kinds of knowledge. Here, then, we seem to have a fundamental basis for distinguishing between differing forms of thinking and understanding, but before we go on to consider how this view has been developed in the context of education and its curriculum implications, let me summarize where we have got to and also make a preliminary point about the nature of freedom and independence of thought on this view.

Summary of rationalism and some implications for freedom of thought

We have been exploring a rationalist view of the nature and development of thought and understanding, and it seems to have the following central characteristics:

1. thinking consists in our organizing experience by defining its different aspects in terms of systems of categories;
2. we do this by judging the ways in which these aspects meet the standards, i.e. rules, which determine what counts as a member of a certain category;
3. these categories form complex webs and theories, and the meaning and value of the different aspects of experience that we articulate by means of them is determined by the place they are allocated in the web;
4. they give structure to living traditions of thought and awareness which form our 'civilized inheritance' and constitute what it is to be human in the full sense;
5. these webs and the procedures that give rise to them and are used to validate them, operate in a way analogous to games: they are governed by rules which are in principle public, and in fact largely shared within a community;
6. it is this public and shared feature of the rules which gives objectivity to the enterprises which they govern, and makes communication possible;
7. each of the distinctive games that it is possible to distinguish constitutes one of the forms that rationality can take.

But what of the following fundamental objection to all this: namely that it presents such a highly convention-based view of thinking that the notion of freedom of thought seems to be quite redundant; that rather than describing the development of an individual's capacity to think, this view presents us with an inhibiting strait-jacket from which thought would need to escape? To this the rationalist seems able to make a number of replies.

The first is that at a very fundamental level without rules of thought there can be no freedom of thought *for there would be no thought at all*. To return to the games analogy: without the rules of the game of football there is no game of football and for someone to claim that their freedom is curtailed by these rules is simply for them to say that they don't wish to play football. Of course, they may wish to change *some* of the rules, but this is to accept the vast majority which form the necessary context against which changes would have a sense, and requires that they gain the agreement of the other players to follow the new rules. Freedom here, then, still consists in following rules, albeit including a limited number of new ones. Indeed, this example shows that freedom consists not in abandoning rules, but precisely in deciding *which rules to follow*. For someone to say they will accept no rules is for them to refuse to play any game, in which case their 'freedom' becomes a commitment to nothing.

Now, in the same way, the rationalist can argue that for someone to say that following rules of thought, i.e. *any* rules of thought, denies their freedom of thought is for them to reject thought altogether (which, of course, they have only been able to do by means of thought) for, if the analogy with games holds here, they are rejecting the basis upon which thought achieves its structure. So here again, freedom consists in following rules, not rejecting them, for it is the rules that provide the different possibilities of thought: different 'games' through which, and between which, we may exercise judgement and choice, and thus express ourselves.

But suppose someone intent upon avoiding the aspect of conventionality that this argument seems to wed to thought were to say: 'Very well, I accept that my freedom of thought is only possible through, and consists in following, rules of thought, but this does not mean that I have to follow the publicly shared ones – I will follow only my own idiosyncratic ones.' While, theoretically, this would no doubt be possible to some degree – and perhaps even then only a relatively small degree, given the background of language learning this decision itself presupposes – such an aspiration would seem to be an expression of pedantry rather than any good sense.

To the extent that an individual succeeded in following only rules that were in fact private, he would have cut himself off from his fellows (since, as we have shown, communication is only possible on the basis of shared rules), and would be unable to avail himself of anything that his culture had produced. His 'freedom' would then consist in thinking in accordance with the very limited and isolated rules he was able to invent for himself and enriched by nothing outside his own narrow experience. Such an end could hardly be the goal of education, nor could it constitute what an educator could mean by the development of independent thought, though the ability to think *beyond* (rather than *without*) currently shared rule structures may be. But this would involve a certain mastery of these rules rather than ignorance of them, and would be the way in which a person working within a culture might extend it. Here, then, inventiveness and creativity, freedom and independence of mind, would occur not through a rejection of shared rules and standards, but on the back of them. The rationalist would claim that through applying and transforming rules within the great public traditions, using the rule-governed critical procedures of these traditions (such as looking for the 'negative instance' in science), veritable quantum shifts in the foundations of thought have been achieved: to wit, the thinking of Copernicus, the 'Enlightenment', Newton, Darwin, Marx and Einstein.

In the presence of such illustrious company, and given the weight of previous argument, would it not be churlish to press the freedom of thought issue any further? And yet. . . .

NOTES AND REFERENCES

1 This account is set out in his paper 'Education: the engagement and its frustration' in Dearden *et al.* (1972).
2 See, for example, H. Lane, *The Wild Boy of Aveyron* (1976). Cambridge, Mass.: Harvard University Press.
3 See Wittgenstein (1958).

CHAPTER 6

Rationality and Liberal Education

We have now considered the main foundations of what I am terming the general rationalist position and it is time to look in a more systematic way at some detailed implications of this view for the development of thinking and understanding in the context of education. Traditionally it has led to what has become known as a 'liberal education', and I propose to consider two versions of this in order to indicate something of the range of views and issues that the rationalist position embraces.

P.H. Hirst: 'Forms of Knowledge' and liberal education

One of the most influential views in the literature of philosophy of education and curriculum theory in recent years is that of Paul Hirst. He has claimed that there exist a number of fundamentally distinct ways of structuring and exploring human experience which constitute the basis for all rational thought, and which are therefore central to the mental development and education of any child. This thesis is, perhaps, so well known that one is hesitant to give yet another exposition of it, but both because of its wide influence and (equally important from our point of view) because of its clear expression of what I have identified as the central themes of rationalism in the educational context, some rehearsal of its main elements is appropriate here.[1] Building on the ideas of Wittgenstein and Oakeshott, and the way in which human activity in its many manifestations can be considered to be rule-governed, Hirst claimed to have distinguished around seven logically distinct forms in the heritage of knowledge and understanding as we have it today. These represent the basic ways in which rationality operates in its endeavour to experience and understand the world, and each, to return to Wittgenstein's analogy, is a 'game' with its own peculiar set of shared rules and standards for doing this. We have already indicated the way in which the activity of science could be seen like this, and indeed science is included – with maths, knowledge of persons, morality, aesthetics, religion and philosophy – on the current list of the forms of knowledge as discerned by Hirst.

Before examining the differentiation of these forms in more detail, it is worth saying something about their nomenclature. They have variously been referred to by Hirst as 'forms of knowledge', 'forms of understanding', 'forms of thought', 'forms of rationality', 'forms of experience', and 'forms of awareness', and while it would perhaps be premature to assume from this that Hirst simply equates these terms, two things are clear: the forms are cognitive/intellectual in character, and all characteristically human experience presupposes them.[2] This thesis, then, unreservedly places the development of the intellect at the centre of the development of the child's consciousness – emotions, attitudes, dispositions, sensitivities etc., all being parasitic on the different forms of intellectual endeavour for their structure. (We might recall here, for example, the section on 'Thought and feeling' in Chapter 2 in which it was suggested that what we feel is heavily dependent upon how we perceive a situation i.e. the beliefs and understandings we bring to bear on it.)

But what is it that individualizes each of the forms? Consistent with the notion of them being forms of intellectual endeavour, each is essentially seen by Hirst as producing its own unique kind of statement about the world and consequently – and this is very important – has its own peculiar method of testing for their truth or falsity. Indeed, for Hirst, how you test for the truth of a statement appears to be closely bound in with its very meaning. He might ask what could even simple statements such as 'The grass is green' or '$2 + 2 = 4$' mean if we had no idea of how to go about checking their truth, i.e. we didn't know what would even *count* as being such a check? This is a central point and we shall examine some of its consequences presently. For the moment we can summarize by saying that each form of knowledge investigates and reveals reality from a unique perspective whose essential character is given by its fundamental concepts and truth tests, and has generated over the course of its historical development conceptual schemes and procedures – i.e. a detailed set of rules – for structuring the whole enterprise.

Let us now consider two examples that seem to match this description quite well. The truth of the statements of mathematics is tested ultimately by reference to whether they can be deduced from certain basic axioms of a particular mathematical system and the statements themselves are founded on certain fundamental concepts which are peculiar to mathematics, such as 'number' or 'matrix'. Though we may teach, say, number bonds through the use of concrete apparatus, the mathematical statement 2 + 2 = 4 is true not because of anything about the physical world, but by definition. If we changed from base 10 to base 3, 2 + 2 would not equal 4, but 11. Counting concrete objects is an *application* of the number system, and while it is certainly true that if we look at: ** ** we see 4 stars, this has no bearing on the mathematical truth of the statement: 2 + 2 = 4 (in base 10). Another way of making this point would be to consider the following situation: Suppose as a result of experimenting with blocks a child were to come up and say 'Look, come and see, I can show you that 2 + 2 = 5'. Would we not know in advance that the child was doing something wrong? As a matter of principle there is nothing he or she could *show* us that would establish the truth of such a claim.

Things stand differently in the realm of science. Here, in contrast to mathematics, the statements of the sciences do make claims about the physical world and therefore are assessed for their truth or falsity not, ultimately, in terms of their compatibility with a pre-specified set of basic definitions, but through their compatibility with observations made through the senses and guided by such fundamental concepts as 'causality', 'energy', 'gravity', 'evolution'. Unlike mathematics, then, scientific understanding constantly changes as a response to new observations of the physical world. It would seem that if something substantially similar can be said about the distinctness of the other members of Hirst's list of forms, he would indeed have identified a number of irreducible ways of making sense of experience and communicating it.

Now the extent to which Hirst is right about this is of the greatest importance with regard to the issue of developing children's thinking, for it goes to the heart of the issue of the basis upon which we make and articulate judgements – the basis upon which we decide what is true or false, good or bad, and communicate this to others. Consider the following statements:

That's a good painting because I like it.
It was a poor film because the hero didn't win.
It's wrong to kick people because it's not allowed here.
It's wrong to hurt people because God said so.
It's not fair that lions eat the other animals.
That's a square because it's coloured blue.
The answer is eight because eight has a nice shape to it.
He looks ugly – he must be wicked.
Plants grow towards the light because Miss Jones says so.
Evolution can't be true because the Bible says so.

Some perhaps have a familiar ring to them, some are understandable, some a little bizarre, but arguably – and I know in some cases this will be contentious – from the point of view of Hirst's thesis they all have something in common wrong with them if taken literally. Taken literally, they each exhibit an inadequacy of judgement, which arises not so much because of having wrong factual information as through applying inappropriate criteria: they refer to the wrong *kind* of evidence – apply the wrong 'test for truth'.

It may be perfectly true that 'Miss Jones said so' but this is not the sort of evidence upon which to base a scientific claim, the fact of someone's being ugly is not an adequate basis for judging their moral character, sheer personal preference is not an adequate basis for judging the aesthetic worth of a painting, and so forth. Often the inadequacy arises, to put it in Hirstian terms, because, embryonically, criteria are being drawn from the wrong form of knowledge: aesthetic to make a moral judgement, religious to make a moral judgement, religious to make a scientific judgement, moral to make an aesthetic judgement, physical or aesthetic properties to make mathematical judgements etc. From the point of view of the forms of knowledge, qualitatively distinct kinds of truth are being hopelessly confused and consequently the very meaning of the statements becomes problematic. What kind of understanding of number and number bonds would a child have who felt that the shape of a number should determine the answer to, say, an addition sum? Thus a vital aspect in developing a child's thinking and understanding will be to help him distinguish between the different kinds of truth and to learn to apply the standards and criteria appropriate to each.

Now there are a number of aspects to this. It will, of course, partly involve acquiring the relevant concepts so as to grasp, for example, that physical properties like colour are not defining characteristics of mathematical shapes, that wild animals are not really the sorts of things to which it is appropriate to apply concepts like fairness. But, as important, it will also involve learning to apply distinct objective procedures, the publicly agreed ways of testing for truth in the area concerned, for surely we are involved in *qualitatively* different kinds of enquiry in, say, deciding the motives for William's invasion of Britain (*knowledge of persons*); what is great about a Beethoven symphony (*aesthetic*); whether one washing powder is better than another (*scientific*); how many prime numbers there are between five and fifty (*mathematical*); whether it's worse to hurt someone than to steal from them (*moral*); how God wants us to live our lives (*religious*); what we mean by 'happiness' or 'freedom' and how important they are compared with, say, being truthful, or responsible (*philosophical*). Attempts to explore experience, make judgements, test ideas, justify views, prove or disprove claims and opinions on such issues involve the use of distinct sets of criteria and standards. To hark back to the analogy of the previous chapter, they are 'games' played by different rules. Thus, to take a recommendation I encountered while attending a teacher in-service course on 'Science across the curriculum', would it not be not merely incongruous, but downright incoherent to write up a scientific experiment as a poem? The distinct qualities which each seeks to exhibit simply seem not to be compatible.

Where, then, do these considerations leave us with regard to the curriculum and the child's education? And what are their implications for the development of children's thinking and in particular their independent thinking? Put simply, if the forms of knowledge are fundamental to thinking and mental development in the way that Hirst describes, it would seem essential to try to initiate every child into each of the forms. Anything less would be to cramp their development in an arbitrary way, to deny them the capacity to enter the full gamut of human understanding and experience which would both enrich their lives and upon which it is necessary ultimately to draw in the making of important practical everyday and larger life decisions. Further, genuine independence of mind (as against mere contra-suggestiveness) and constructive imagination and creativity, would be achieved by learning to play these fundamental 'knowledge games': i.e. learning the characteristic forms of expression, conceptual schemes, truth tests, and procedures for each of the forms. For only upon this basis would an individual be able to assess the claims of others and generate his or her own understanding – as against being the passive receiver of other's views – and only on this basis could his or her imagination and creativity receive rational structure.

This last point is of utmost importance. Contrary to what sometimes seems to be assumed in discussions about the purposes of education, on Hirst's view there can be no *general* mental powers – such as, say, the capacity to think logically, or critically or creatively – which could simply be developed in their own right. Like all other aspects of thought, mental powers must derive their structure from the particular form of rationality within which they are operating: there is mathematical creativity, scientific creativity, philosophical creativity etc., but not general creative power *as such*, unless this term is simply used summatively to refer to a person's having developed a number of distinct creative capacities. Being critical, creative, ingenious etc., is a very different activity from one form to another because they are structured by different sets of procedures and standards and we would be quite wrong to assume, then, that the development of these capacities in one area will transfer to another. People could be, and some are, creative mathematicians and pedantic poets.

Of course, to acknowledge the existence of such distinct forms of knowledge is neither to say that they may not interrelate, nor that necessarily they should be taught in separate timetable slots. To take the first point, whilst it may be true that one might have a rich aesthetic experience of, say, a sunset quite independently of any scientific understanding of it in terms of refraction of light rays etc., and vice versa, it is equally true that a great deal of our more developed scientific understanding would not be possible without an understanding of some aspects of mathematics. Similarly, moral judgements clearly often require knowledge and understanding drawn from other areas such as the physical sciences and knowledge of persons. With regard to the second point, we have already noticed in Chapter 3 how certain traditional school subjects such as English and geography draw on a number of what would count as different forms of knowledge in Hirst's terms. The fact that such 'combinations' of ways of thinking have a long tradition and have been valued over a substantial period of time suggests that they are not merely arbitrary conglomerations.

But, now, if it is true some forms of knowledge draw on others, and if it has been found valuable to combine a number of forms in exploring certain areas of experience, does it not begin to seem that the forms are not as logically distinct as Hirst supposes? In which case would not serious doubt be cast over the claim that they are the fundamental forms that thought and understanding take, and therefore over their status as the basic planning units of curriculum structure, setting its basic objectives?

Such a line of argument would, however, seem to be too hasty. That one form of knowledge *utilizes* another in no way affects the claim that one cannot be *reduced* to the other. Hirst would argue that no matter how prominent maths may become in science, there will always be something uniquely scientific which maths cannot replace and *to which the maths has become subservient*. The motivation underlying the use of mathematical statements in this context is the pursuit of scientific truth, not mathematical truth. Similarly, that certain combinations of the forms have proved themselves valuable or convenient in human affairs over a sustained period of time, is not necessarily to deny that they are indeed combinations – that is, of distinct elements – and perhaps represents a good illustration of how human problems and decision-making are dependent upon the forms.

Such considerations, then, should lead to the rejection of any quick assumption that on Hirst's view the forms should be taught in isolation from each other. Whether this should be so would depend on all manner of considerations concerning how children learn best in the differing circumstances in which teaching is

63

taking place. Because of the considerable variation in individual children's levels of ability and styles of learning, and in the contexts of learning, it would be unwise to expect that there could be any one universal recipe or prescription here. But whatever methods and kind of curriculum organization are considered, the basic purpose, objectives, and criteria of success would remain clear: *their effectiveness as a means to enabling pupils to acquire the rules, standards, and procedures that constitute the distinct forms of knowledge* such that they would be able to begin to operate within these forms and structure their own experience in terms of them. Only in this way would they achieve rational consciousness and gain objective understanding of themselves and their environment. And this is the essence of the traditional notion of liberal education: a mind liberated from ignorance and freed to explore reality in a rational manner.

Here, then, we are given very considerable guidance as to what the achievements are that constitute the development of thought and understanding, and therefore what the general compass and more specific goals of the curriculum should be. And since a proper grasp of these considerations will clearly be beyond the pupils themselves, the view would seem to lend support to the notion of an extensive pre-specified compulsory curriculum whose main objectives would be set out by those who had mastered the various forms of rationality that our culture has so far produced.

Such a view clearly informs a good deal of current thinking and policy-making in education. It also seems to me to draw very faithfully the consequences for education of those basic tenets of rationalism that I have previously described, particularly in the way it orientates education around the development of intellectual understanding in its various forms and its emphasis on the public nature of this understanding conferred by its underlying structure of impersonal rules, standards, and procedures, whose aspiration is the achievement of objective truth.

Because of its faithfulness to these defining characteristics of rationality – both in the view of knowledge and understanding it advocates and its heavy emphasis on logical analysis, even when this leads to conclusions that are counter-intuitive, in arriving at this view – I will term it a version of 'hard rationalism'. Its main strength is that it gives a systematic account of the different forms that understanding may take, which, if correct, would provide a clear and fundamental set of considerations to be brought to bear in thinking about how to structure the curriculum. But its great strength is also its great weakness. In attempting to describe the whole realm of human understanding as being the product of rationality, and in attempting to organize its different facets in accordance with a common model of rationality, it seems to run into severe dangers of distorting at least some of the areas it purports to be characterizing.

The main source of this distortion is Hirst's determination to characterize thought and understanding as ultimately revolving around the notion of making statements whose meaning is largely a function of the objective tests for truth used to verify them. The problem here is that many areas of thought that intuitively one feels to be of great value and to be integral – indeed, *defining* – aspects of the human condition do not sit happily under this description. The idea that the arts make statements in a way analogous to, say, maths or science or morality, and that these statements can be judged as true or false, just does not seem to mesh with our experience in this area. The question as to, say, what statement the *Mona Lisa* makes, and whether it is true, seems quite inappropriate, and in any case hardly seems to characterize the essence of aesthetic contemplation. This is a crucial point for the hard rationalist, suggesting as it does that even if a fuller account than, as a matter of fact, Hirst has yet provided of the objective tests for truth for each of the forms was forthcoming (he has been conspicuously vague on this point in areas such as aesthetics, morality, religion), they might be of no, or limited, relevance in characterizing many of the most fundamental domains of thought and understanding achieved by human civilization.

The seriousness of this dilemma in terms of the hard rationalist's attempt to provide an important part of the rationale for the curriculum is illustrated by the three possible responses that seem left to them. Firstly, they may simply insist that the arts *are* centrally concerned to make statements, but we have yet to properly understand and describe the way in which this is so. But this stance rests on a quite unwarranted article of faith, denying one of the basic rationalist tenets of basing belief on good reason, and must surely be treated as simply an unsubstantiated and implausible claim until the required demonstration of its truth is provided.

Secondly, they may allow that the making of statements is only one aspect of the arts, and possibly not its central one. But this would surely be to deny the original thesis that the forms of knowledge are the source of mental structures and conscious awareness, since it is to concede that in the arts at least there is experience which lies outside and independently of them. It would also mean that one would not turn to the forms of knowledge thesis in setting out objectives in this area, since to teach the arts in the way they appear from the perspective of this thesis would be highly distorting.

Lastly the hard rationalist may say that the arts do not, essentially, make statements and are therefore not forms of rational thought – and therefore not proper components of a liberal education. Such a response would at least be consistent with the original premises of the theory. But it has the consequence of leading to a cabined and unattractive view of education, resulting from dogma rather than genuine openness to the nature and range of the achievements which have come to define human consciousness and potential.

Partly in response to such criticisms, more recently a view of education has been expressed which, while derived from the same basic tenets, could be construed as giving them a 'softer' interpretation than Hirst, and thereby provides an interesting alternative. Since it could be seen as avoiding some of the less attractive features and more obvious difficulties which attach to hard rationalism, we will turn to it now as a means of rounding out our view of the rationalist perspective on the development of thinking and understanding in the educational context.

Charles Bailey: Beyond the present and the particular[3]

Charles Bailey, who has clearly been influenced by all the writers we have so far considered, seeks to provide a view of liberal education based on a rationality which he feels to be less abstracted from human experience than that of Hirst. Taking up the criticism that Hirst's tendency to dwell on what he perceives to be strictly logical considerations runs the danger of seriously distorting the character of the activities which they purport to describe, Bailey advocates a notion of liberal education – and therefore rational development of mind – formed on a different basis.

Taking up a distinction made by Oakeshott, Bailey claims that human experience is subject to a duality of two worlds: the world of persons, and the world of physical material and structures. Thus, and in contrast to Hirst, he claims that there are only two fundamentally distinct forms of understanding: one that focuses on exhibition of intelligence, i.e. any form of human practice; another that focuses on aspects of the purely physical world. For Bailey, this is the only fundamental logical division within the domain of knowledge, such other divisions as exist being matters of tradition or convenience. Furthermore, he wishes to maintain that these forms, particularly the former, are concerned with a much richer notion of meaning than that expressed in statements and derived from their tests for truth. He points out that the notion of meaning has many more senses than the hard rationalist seems to allow, or at least is prepared to celebrate. For example, in addition to the meaning given by having some understanding of how we test for the truth of things – important as this is – there is meaning in the sense of understanding the intention of an utterance or piece of behaviour (for example, was it intended as compliment or insult?), its personal point or significance ('You've got the job!'), its importance ('The King is dead') and purpose (for example, to induce a sense of self-worth or bring about a change in behaviour). The point is that there is a richness of meanings, any and each of which can, on occasion, be of the highest importance, which the formal notion of statement-making alone cannot encompass.

Thus Bailey gives a view of the development of thought and understanding which is not tied to the different classes of statements it may be possible to make. But if it is not to be based on this, what is it to be based on? Clearly, while the duality of understanding thesis may be very important, it is hardly sufficient to the task of describing the content of a liberal education. How are we to select within the two great domains of understanding so as to produce a curriculum which is both balanced and conveys what is centrally important?

Bailey makes a start on this problem by providing a list of principles upon which, in his view, the structure of a liberal education should be founded. I pick out some of the main ones below.[4] A liberal education should be:

(1) liberating from the restrictions of the present and the particular;
(2) concerned with knowledge and understanding which is fundamental and has general applicability;
(3) concerned with intrinsically valued ends;
(4) concerned with the development of reason;
(5) concerned with what is objectively valuable, that is, what is justifiably to be valued.

Such a list clearly gives the impression of a more broadly based view of liberal education than the hard rationalist, for example it seems to suggest that the development of reason is now only one end amongst others. But on this point, such an impression is, I suspect, erroneous.

Let us consider each of the principles in a little more detail. The first is of prime importance, providing as it does the title for Bailey's book. But what does it mean to be 'liberated from the restrictions of the present and the particular'? Bailey seems to have in mind here the development of a person's capacity to stand back from his or her immediately present situation, locate it in a wider framework of understanding, and thus be placed to some degree in the position of being able to make autonomous choices with regard to it. This is clearly a very important (for some, almost a defining) human capacity and what seems to lie at the heart of it is one of the basic motives of rationality which we identified in Chapter 4: the desire to assess and evaluate, and which, as we saw in our discussion there, is a function of the basic categorizing activity in which rationality consists. We 'liberate' ourselves from what is immediately present by seeing things as instances of more general categories.

This connects with the second of Bailey's principles. The generalizable knowledge and understanding which he envisages are clearly also an expression of this categorizing activity: fundamentality of understanding refers to the acquisition of categories which are of greater generality, and therefore applicability. Thus, for example, concepts such as 'ritual' or 'authority' can be applied across a wider range of situations and societies than those of 'shaking hands' or 'police constable'.

That Bailey should be concerned with knowledge and understanding which is 'objectively valuable' is bound to be the case, since the central aspiration of any rationalist account is the achievement of objective truth arrived at through shared forms of reasoning. And finally, that liberal education must be concerned with intrinsically valued ends would seem to follow from this: in the end reasoning must come to rest on those things which are to be valued for their own sake and in the service of which other things become means. It is important to recognize that it is an understanding of the intrinsically valuable which is of the most fundamental kind, for it is this that gives direction to, and overarches, all else. We have ultimately to decide what our underlying purposes are – i.e. which things we value for themselves – in order properly to decide our priorities and the most appropriate means to achieving them.

As we go through Bailey's principles, then, it becomes clear that he is not attempting to give an account of liberal education which goes beyond the concerns of rationality, rather he is attempting to give an enriched notion of rationality itself.

What sort of curriculum would this more generous conception of rationality suggest, and what will be the basis of its justification once we move away from the objectivity that strict logical analysis is supposed to provide? The spirit of what Bailey wants is conveyed in the following quotation:

> Education, in its liberating sense, is appropriate for persons because only persons act out of their *own understandings* of situations they find themselves in. They do not simply react or live out built-in instincts or behaviour patterns. Persons enter a world already perceived through the understandings, meanings and practices shaped and modified by countless generations of persons before them, and these understandings have themselves to be understood by young persons, not merely received as passed on to them. This is the vision, and to manage this with integrity is the task of liberal education.[5]

The detail is roughly as follows. In the primary years of schooling emphasis should be placed on the development of what he terms the 'serving competencies' of literacy, numeracy, logical reasoning, physical education, and also certain dispositions (an area not explicitly considered by Hirst), such as to attend, concentrate, co-operate, reason, inquire, imagine, etc. For Bailey, these are all a necessary prerequisite for the attainment of the larger goals of a liberal education, including entrance to those 'two great orders of inquiry': understanding of human practices, and understanding of physical material and structures. But now, how are we to specify a content within these two great orders if we do not admit any logical divisions within them of the kind that Hirst did? It seems that we must be content with a justification of somewhat 'softer' objectivity.

In the case of inquiry into human practices we are to seek those long-established divisions which historically and/or anthropologically have been valuable in 'the developing understanding of their situation by human beings'. Interestingly, and contra Hirst, Bailey makes it clear he does not mean by this that the value of these understandings is necessarily to be judged in terms of their objective truth, it is rather the extent to which such understandings have been of significance in human history and development. For example, if we took the area of religious practices and understanding, we could believe its claims to be false but still argue for its inclusion in a liberal education on the grounds of its large influence historically, and across different cultures, on the understanding and practices of human beings. In the case of the field of inquiry into the physical world, the criterion is in some ways parallel, but embodies a significant difference. The content is selected in terms of its importance in developing understanding of oneself as a physical organism in relation to other organisms inhabiting a physical universe. Here there seems to be more emphasis on the notion of truth in that presumably Bailey wishes what is taught about the physical world to be warranted by the current state of the evidence, and would thus preclude astrology even though, like religion, it has been of enduring and widespread influence.

On the basis of the criteria set out above Bailey advocates a pretty extensive compulsory curriculum. To the serving competencies already mentioned, we must now add the 'humanities proper' (literature, history, morality, religion), and inquiries into the 'makings and practices of persons' (including their social, political, economic, industrial, and commercial institutions; mathematical and logical systems; religion and morality; art, craft and design; literature and drama; music and dance; games and physical activities). And this must be complemented by an equally long list of topics and areas of understanding of the physical world (for example: the workings of the human body; health, medicine, nutrition; the behaviour and ecology of plants and animals; simple technologies; astronomy and cosmology; physical geography and meteorology; energy and material resources; ecology and conservation). With so demanding a compulsory curriculum in mind, Bailey's suggestion that, in response to certain child-centred considerations, 'there is no reason why schools should not (also) have facilities for offering all kinds of activities and studies to be chosen on the basis of personal interest' must appear, at first blush, somewhat tongue in cheek.

However, Bailey's soft rationalism has certainly come up with a rich view of what it is to be liberally educated, and the way it attempts to firmly root itself in the needs of a person in interaction with the social and physical world is attractive when compared with the rather abstract feel of hard rationalism. It is certainly more likely to meet the demands for relevance to 'real life' that are sometimes made by the recipients of education, and by teachers who both think it important for children to see a point in what they are doing, and appreciate the motivational advantages of their doing so. But is it sufficiently well founded? That is to say, has it shown with sufficient stringency what constitutes the different activities that it lists as contributing to our understanding of ourselves in relation to the world and the rationale for this particular listing? This is an important issue to clarify: if we are to avoid a very content-led curriculum we need a firmer sense of what it will be to engage with the topics listed and precisely what they have to offer to the development of children's thinking.

For example, within each of the two great orders of inquiry are there different thought games, or only one with differing contents? What place, if any, would be given to the disciplines of history, geography, philosophy, psychology and sociology in, say, the inquiries into the makings and practices of persons? And

71

what emphasis would be given to learning their own procedures and ways of organizing and explaining things? Indeed, are the lists themselves as much the result of applying some kind of implicit wisdom as of applying the explicitly stated criteria? For example, why not microbiology or architecture instead of astronomy? And finally, on a somewhat different tack, does Bailey's whole view of the curriculum, as with that of hard rationalism, too readily jump from the claim that something is objectively valuable to the conclusion that it should therefore be compulsory – motivational problems then being not matters of choice of content, but problems only of method? A more thorough consideration of the strengths and weaknesses of 'hard' and 'soft' rationalism, and their consequences for teaching, is the business of the next chapter, but before moving on to this it will be useful to briefly consider the perspectives these views offer on another important issue.

Education and 'the basics'

Closely associated with the issue of standards in education which we discussed in Chapter 2 has been the issue of the extent to which primary education should focus on 'the basics'. A perennially recurring criticism over recent years has been that the basics are receiving too little systematic attention in the primary curriculum and this has a seriously debilitating effect not only on the general standard of performance of children in primary schools but also in their ability to cope with secondary education and the demands of life outside school. And again, as with the 'standards' debate, protagonists of this view have tended to operate with a largely unexamined set of assumptions about what the basics are. They have taken it as self-evident that they were to be pretty well equated with the '3Rs' – thought of largely in terms of factual knowledge such as multiplication tables and spellings and relatively mechanical skills such as word recognition, punctuation, handwriting and numerical computation.

Now, of course even at this level of debate real problems are in danger of being glossed over, notwithstanding the fact that some are now very familiar. For example, in the age of cheap calculators is it really speed of computation or understanding of number operations that is basic: in what likely situations today would someone do 'manually' a series of extensive long division sums? Problems connected with what is basic to becoming a reader have been illustrated in the previously mentioned discussion on educational standards (p. 18). But the real issue with regard to the 'basics' derives from the fact that what counts as basic is dependent upon a perception of what is needed. And this clearly involves reference to an underlying, if often implicit, set of values. Is it usefulness in everyday life that should be the criterion? Or what will be needed for future education? Or what? If we take everyday utility as the justification for concentrating on the 3Rs, it is interesting to ask just how much of them does it support? Exactly what *level* of word recognition, spelling etc. is 'basic'? This is an important curriculum issue if the force of labelling something as 'basic' is to give it priority over other things in terms of time and resources.

Clearly also, we should need to keep abreast of changing social and technological circumstances, for example – extending the 'calculator' theme – what effect should the likely availability in the foreseeable future of cheap, portable word processors with spell checks have on our perception of the 'basicness' of certain language aspects of the 3Rs? And to move on to a more recent candidate for treatment as a basic, how much of the National Curriculum 'core subject' Science can be said to be absolutely necessary to get by in everyday life? In our technological age, the very complexity and sophistication of the machines and instruments that we commonly use and the consequent proliferation of 'black boxes' in our practical lives give a strong impetus to rely on experts rather than our own scientific understanding of the things we use. Understanding and soldering up a broken crystal radio receiver is one thing, but a Nicam television set?. . . a computer?. . . CD car ignition?

Further, what is to be meant by 'getting by in life' anyway? Doesn't this beg all sorts of questions about the quality of life we hope or expect to lead? If we mean something like surviving in modern society, not only do many people in 'average' occupations seem to get by remarkably well with little or no systematic scientific understanding (including, it might be noted, plumbers and garage mechanics), but also so do many highly successful professionals. The underlying point here is that the quality of life we may desire is shaped by our outlook – our view of what life is and how it could and should be led – and this in turn is significantly shaped by our education. Thus what is considered to be basic in education is perhaps more appropriately linked to the intrinsic aims of education itself, that is to say, the question becomes: what things are basic to achieving the larger substantive goals of education?

Now if we take this stance clearly it will be important to make as clear as possible what our underlying concept of education is. This is where the two views of liberal education we have been considering provide food for thought. They pose the question: 'What are the basic prerequisites for achieving liberation from ignorance and the full development of the rational mind?' If this latter is conceived basically in terms of initiation into the logically distinct forms of knowledge, then it is possible that a much enriched view of the basics will begin to emerge.

To begin with, acquisition of central concepts, procedures and ways of testing for truth in each of these forms will be basic and will be of equal priority. (Thus there would be no 'core' subjects as with the National Curriculum.) And the 3Rs themselves would be treated differently. For example, in mathematics the emphasis would move away from computational skills to understanding number operations and developing broader mathematical concepts such as those of 'set' and 'matrix', which arguably are basic to understanding so much else in that area. Reading and writing, once they rose above the relatively mechanical level of word recognition and forming one's letters to the grasping and expression of meanings, would truly require a 'language across the curriculum' approach, for if, as Hirst claims, meaning is embedded within the different forms, literacy must itself involve engagement with the conceptual structures and sets of procedures that constitute them. There can be no notion of reading as a *general* skill which of itself will enable the child to read with understanding across the forms of knowledge. To read with understanding is precisely to engage with the concepts peculiar to each of them. Thus the 'basics' of reading and writing on this view becomes the ability to engage intelligently with material within each of the separate forms. This raises interesting issues concerning the kinds and range of reading material in terms of which children's reading should be developed and assessed.

Similarly, Charles Bailey's version of a liberal education invites a much enriched view of what counts as the basics, his notion of the 'serving competencies'[6] acknowledging a range of skills and dispositions which far outstrips the 3Rs. We have noted how, alongside fairly conventional notions of literacy and numeracy he places:

> logical reasoning – to be able to infer, avoid contradiction, to hypothesize, to discern what is logically possible and what is not;
> to think critically;
> physical fitness;

and, importantly, a range of dispositions such as:

> to attend;
> to concentrate;
> to co-operate;
> to organize time, material, thought and action;
> to reason;
> to imagine possibilities;
> to inquire – try to understand.

On Bailey's view these are all instrumental to serving the larger purposes of a liberal education and suggest a set of priorities which go way beyond traditional conceptions of the basics in terms of what they imply for the experiences that the primary curriculum should be providing for children.

While I am not here going to argue in detail the merits or otherwise of these views, I suggest that claims of this kind certainly need to be taken very seriously. They serve to provoke a more thoughtful assessment as to what the basics in primary education really are, along with what could be far-reaching implications for establishing priorities within the curriculum. And broad policy decisions about the basics apart, Hirst's emphasis on central concepts and procedures, and Bailey's emphasis on what is more fundamental and generalizable might provide useful criteria in deciding priorities when faced with a plethora of National Curriculum objectives – in which distinctions of kind and underlying value are not usually made explicit.

Take the vast content potential of, say, a topic on the Aztecs. Sympathy with rationalists such as Hirst and Bailey would incline us to give greater emphasis to objectives that required understanding rather than, say, recall of information, or the naming of parts, and to aspects of Aztec society which could exemplify concepts transferable to understanding other societies such as 'ritual', 'adaption to environment', 'culture' or 'way of life' rather than very context-specific items such as the names of items of clothing, the location of towns, or particular customs taught for their own sake. One might also look carefully at the opportunities provided by the topic for exercising capacities for thinking logically, critically, independently; for hypothesizing, translating, interpreting, evaluating etc., and the sorts of situations and questions one might need to frame to provoke them. The central argument here is that the particularities of, say, Aztec life may be fascinating in themselves, but treated in this way such particularities may become the vehicle for developing a range of ideas and capacities which are basic to understanding so much else besides. And what could be wrong with this?

NOTES AND REFERENCES

1   See, particularly, Hirst (1965). See also Hirst and Peters (1972), *The Logic of Education*, Ch. 4. But also see Hirst (1993) for what looks like a repudiation of some of his own previously held views (not that any change of heart on his part affects the arguments being developed in this chapter).
2   As Hirst put it in *The Logic of Education* (p. 62): 'there can be no experience or knowledge without the acquisition of the relevant concepts. Further, it is only when experience and thought, which necessarily involve the use of concepts of some sort, involve those shared in a public world, that the achievements with which we are concerned are possible.'
      This view was itself foreshadowed by Peters (1966, pp. 48–9): 'The ideas and expectations of an individual centre of consciousness . . . are the product of the initiation of an individual into public traditions enshrined in the language, concepts, beliefs, and rules of a society.' Prior to this: 'His "mind" is ruled perhaps by bizarre and formless wishes in which there is no picking out of objects . . .'
3   The views expressed here are taken from his book *Beyond the Present and the Particular: A Theory of Liberal Education* (1983).
4   Ibid. The full list is to be found on p. 105.
5   Ibid., p. 107.
6   Ibid., pp. 110–14.

CHAPTER 7

Rationality and Education Reconsidered

We have now considered the way in which rationalism conceives the development of thought and understanding in the context of education, both in general terms and in its 'hard' and 'soft' manifestations. But how adequate an account of thinking and understanding does rationalism give, and how acceptable are its broader implications for teaching? We have already noted that rationalism characterizes thought as highly dependent upon public conventions for its structure and objectivity, and I intend to begin my evaluation by considering this aspect in a little more depth. Let us begin with some of its strengths.

Education, objectivity, and public standards

It seems to me to be quite correct to suppose that to develop someone's thinking is to somehow improve it. And to improve it is to say that it has now achieved some new, higher standard which is in some sense objective. Certainly this element of objectivity is of great importance in the educational situation, for without it judgements of progress will be arbitrary and the idea of educating someone unintelligible. For example, if no objectivity attaches to the judgement that reading Tolstoy is superior to reading the *Dandy* – if, at bottom, this is simply a matter of subjective whim – then the notion of making progress in the area of a child's appreciation of literature, i.e. of educating in this area, falls apart, for there could be no cause to wean him or her off the *Dandy* onto anything else which is more demanding. (And surely it *is* the case that within the field of children's literature itself, *Tom's Midnight Garden* by Philippa Pearce, for example, is more demanding, more perceptive, more refining of emotion and outlook – thus better literature and more educative in some objective sense, than the comic strip *Desperate Dan*?)

Now there is a response to this sort of issue, often strongly voiced, which in my view is as misguided and damaging as it is pervasive and tempting. It runs something like this: it does not follow that a teacher needs objective values, for we could have as our educational objective the idea of helping children to make their own informed choices. Such an aim, it might be argued, need make no reference to any notion of objective standards of quality in the arts since it simply seeks to broaden the base upon which a child will make up his or her own mind on such matters. Judgements of quality and value in this area, and perhaps in many others, are ultimately subjective, and to encourage children to see some things as of higher quality or more value than others, is to indoctrinate.

This way of thinking clearly has a great initial attraction: it seems liberal in outlook, and to relieve us of the often difficult task of trying to identify, articulate and demonstrate to the satisfaction of others, the objectivity of what we take to be of value. The difficulty of this is so notorious in some areas, such as the arts, that there can be an almost overwhelming temptation to say values here are purely subjective: 'Beauty lies in the eye of the beholder.' On a broader front, in a situation of cultural diversity and pluralism of moral and social values that exists in many schools, this appeal to some form of relativism seems to grow in strength. But can it be the proper function of the primary school simply and indescriminately to reinforce across the board whatever values a child may bring? I wish to suggest that despite its undeniable attractiveness, such relativism is a temptation to which we should not, and probably as educators cannot, succumb. Since I believe this to be a crucial, though sometimes unrecognized issue for teaching, I will develop it a little further here.

The first point that must be made is that any course of action involves commitment to a value, which is at the very least to treat it *as if* it were objective. So the teacher who believes that the imposition of value-judgements can be avoided in the area of children's literature by bringing children to a point where they can make their own informed choice is herself committed at least to this – the value of informed choice. Secondly, it may seem possible in many roles to live in the spirit of the subjectivist thesis, but in the role of teacher, where one has explicit responsibility to guide the development of others, its problems are insurmountable and the intellectual self-deception it involves is likely to lead to bad practice. Teachers cannot avoid making decisions about what to do, the direction they will encourage learning to take, and they will be exhibiting values throughout the whole gamut of their behaviour, from their way of relating to children in general, to particular qualities of work they do and do not praise, to their approaches to discipline and class control, and so forth. To return to the example given above: decisions concerning what is to count as a broad base of understanding, and what counts as representative of different styles in literature, will involve many tacit values, which are being treated as if they are objective. The subjectivist outlook will leave all this largely implicit and unexamined – for what could be the point of doing otherwise, if ultimately anything is as good as anything else? But if the teacher will be endorsing certain values nonetheless by virtue of her guiding role, surely we are entitled to require that the values being endorsed are made clear, and to ask whether they are worthy ones?

Honest subjectivism would lead to paralysis or chaos: the former, in the sense that there would be no basis for making any choices (even to choose to do something purely out of whim, is to be committed to the value of doing *this*); the latter, in the sense that we are then left only with a world of mindless reaction. There is an important sense in which the human condition is *characterized* by its capacity to value. And unlike simply desiring something, valuing it means that we attribute some quality to it which is not purely the product of personal whim, but has some objective basis. That is to say that internal to the meaning of valuing is some notion of properness, fittingness, appropriateness, of the thing valued which belongs to it independently of our caprice. It is experienced as a facet of the situated thing itself and is therefore something that strictly speaking we discern, rather than simply decide. Thus thorough-going subjectivism is not merely a view about the nature of values, it is a view whose consequence is a denial that there are such things as values. And in so doing, it denies an essential aspect of what it is to be human.

The truth of the matter is, I think, that often those who say that all values are subjective (or relative) in the kinds of situations we have been considering, do so out of the best of motives, but on the basis of a confusion which actually works against what they seek. Concerns not to indoctrinate or to foist off values on pupils are not based on subjectivism, but on a positive commitment to such things as the individual subjectivity of pupils, the integrity of differing cultures and the value of tolerance. In other words, it is a commitment to a set of values that we might loosely call those of a liberal democracy – which may or may not be reflected in the home background of a particular child. To be so committed is not to believe that any values are as good as any others, but that in some objective sense liberal democratic values are more justifiable than others.

But what, then, is the source of objectivity in our judgements of value? Could it not be at this point that the notion of public conventions emphasized by rationalism has an important part to play, for is it not largely in terms of sets of criteria that have evolved throughout the period of human beings' interaction with the various aspects of their environment that judgements of worth are made? These would seem to escape the purely arbitrary through having become widely agreed and shared. The notion that objectivity is achieved by reference to shared rules, or conventions, seems to allow the possibility of objective judgement in areas which otherwise would be hard-pressed to rise above the purely arbitrary (thus placing them beyond the pale of education), and invites a more generous and sensitive conception of truth than might otherwise be possible. There has been a tendency in modern times to equate objectivity with *scientific* objectivity, and as a result areas of thought and understanding, such as the arts and humanities, which cannot produce the hard 'proof' for their claims that science is often characterized as doing, have sometimes come to be regarded as merely subjective, inferior, or even illusory. But if we allow that objectivity and truth result from the application of publicly agreed criteria, then it would seem that there can be as many kinds of truth as there are sets of conventions (or 'knowledge games', to use the terminology of a previous chapter), and the imperialism of science is broken. This could be seen as both liberating and status-restoring to non-scientific studies, which would no longer be pushed into regarding themselves as poor imitations of something else. Interestingly, though, this possibility, which is so conspicuous in the hard rationalism of Hirst, appears somewhat restricted in the soft rationalism of Bailey, which allows of only two logically distinct modes of thought – despite Bailey's wish to provide an enriched view of rationality.

Another upshot of rationalism's emphasis on public convention in the structuring of thought is that it holds out the prospect of being able to set out objectively justifiable goals which would constitute what is to count as progress in the development of children's thought in the different areas. By careful analysis of each of the knowledge games it should be possible to identify agreed key concepts, propositions, and procedures and set these out in a graded way from the relatively simple to the relatively complex. Such an approach appears to be the basis of many maths and science schemes in use in schools today, and seems to hold the important benefit of both providing a coherent programme of work in the area concerned, and an objective means of monitoring achievement. If this could be applied to other areas of the curriculum (and why should it not be, if they, too, consist in sets of public concepts?) this would seem to be an important step towards developing children's thinking and understanding in these areas in the most efficient way. The hierarchical structure of 'levels' and 'key stages' of the National Curriculum reflects an attempt to pursue this approach on the grand scale.

A further consequence of the view that thinking is structured by shared conventions and agreed standards of truth, quality and value, is that claims made in the different areas of understanding will be assessable in terms of the publicly accepted reasons or evidence given to support them. Indeed, on this view, what it is to *have* an understanding of something will largely be to have acquired the public evidence and reasoning upon which claims concerning it are based. Thus a child's understanding of, say, how plants grow would be developed by providing explanations on two fronts: (a) explanation of the public meaning of the terms used to describe this process; (b) explanation of the supporting evidence. Rationalism constantly draws our attention beyond the question of '*What* do you know?' to the question of '*How* do you know?', and insists that both must be answered in accordance with publicly accepted standards.

In sum, the task of the teacher, then, is to convey public meanings and evidence, and this will involve an on-going process of de-centring on the part of the child as her thinking develops by being confronted with considerations other than those that derive from her own affectively conditioned and impressionistic outlook, and becomes organized around sets of impersonal public standards. As R.S. Peters once put it, the rational thinker is one who takes on the perspective of the 'generalized other'.[1] In this way, through the internalization of such impersonal public standards and their application in her experience, the child will come to perceive and believe in a way that is *justifiable*, i.e. does not contravene the rules of the relevant 'game', and takes account of the available evidence.

It can be seen, then, that rationalism seems to provide a set of answers (some of which have been set out in more detail in previous chapters) to many of the most pressing questions that face a teacher who is seriously concerned to develop a child's thinking and capacity to understand. It gives an account of the way in which thinking is structured, the importance and source of any objectivity it may achieve, the extent to which it takes radically different forms and what such differences consist in, and what would be centrally involved in being critical, creative, and capable of independent thought. It also gives suggestions for the broad framework of a curriculum intended to develop pupil's thinking, and something of the content which would flesh this out.

However, its attempt to provide this guidance is not without its problems, some of which begin to surface in the tension between what I have termed 'hard' and 'soft' rationalism. One of the problems highlighted there is that just as hard rationalism provides relatively sharp criteria for the distinctions it claims at the price of plausibility in many areas, so soft rationalism recaptures some plausibility at the price of lack of sharp distinctions and justification. That rationalism presents us with a choice between, on the one hand, a view that is vitiated by its attempt to be objective and precise, and on the other hand a view that is vitiated by its attempt to stay in touch with experience, perhaps suggests that it is not wholly adequate to the task it has set itself. We will return to this possibility in Part Three. For the moment, there are some other reservations to express.

Rationalism and the subjective dimension

To begin with, a point needs to be raised about the general description of thinking as being articulated by rules. We must beware of being seduced by the apparent simplicity of this account and the promise that it seems to hold out of being able to specify all aspects of thinking – as if thinking and understanding are basically matters of knowing the appropriate recipes which, presumably, once properly identified, could be systematically taught. To what extent could this be true? It would clearly be important to establish this in relation to the different areas of teaching. It would also be important to note the following point: even in those areas where an emphasis on rule-following seems applicable, *applying* a rule often involves far more than simply *knowing* a rule. Take such basic rules as 'sentences end with a full stop' or 'you start a new paragraph when you go on to a new point'. Such rules are perhaps acceptable as far as they go, but clearly they beg the real questions. How does the child tell exactly when to end a sentence, or exactly what counts as a significant change of point? What further rules could we adduce to settle such matters? Ultimately, don't we just have to *sense* such things – develop a feel for the nature of the content we are dealing with? This notion of 'sensing' seems to reintroduce into the account something far more complex, subjective and perhaps ultimately non-rational, that preoccupation with knowing rules can obscure. This is a matter to which we will return presently.

Secondly, I think that a strong criticism can be made with regard to the rationalist's assumption that to have shown that an area of thinking has objective value carries the consequence that it must therefore be compulsory. This seems to embody an imperialism of the most strident kind, for though I have argued that value is not simply arbitrary, it is nonetheless *contextual*. That is to say, it is bound up with the particularities of differing, and in many ways, unique situations. Thus we may say, for example, that given a certain situation, an understanding of some aspect of science *is* valuable in the objective sense that we are claiming this to be true for all relevantly similar situations. But this, of course, is not to presume that everyone is in, or will find themselves in, such a situation. This would be a further claim yet to be demonstrated, and to make wholesale assumptions about it is both arrogant and absurd. Einstein's theory of relativity is doubtless of great objective value, but that hardly warrants a claim that it should be compulsory learning for all children. Something's being of objective value at most implies that it is of potential rather than actual value to any individual at any particular time.

Such considerations concerning the nature of objectivity, and its relationship with notions of a compulsory curriculum, bring us starkly up against the way rationalistic approaches to the development of thinking and understanding tend to disregard motivational aspects of learning. It is not, of course, that a teacher persuaded of this kind of view will be insensitive to the benefits of presenting what has to be learnt in as interesting and enjoyable a form as possible, but that for such a teacher this comes essentially as an afterthought – something one tries to do with or to a content which has already been chosen on other grounds. Thus Charles Bailey claims that:

> problems of motivation are not essentially problems of choice of content, but methodological and strategical problems of pedagogy concerned with how to engage pupils in what is demonstrably worthwhile.[2]

But, quite apart from the fact that this puts a quite impossible burden of responsibility on the shoulders of a teacher to make what he or she is teaching interesting to all pupils – which, if taken seriously, could only lead to feelings of guilt and frustration on a fairly massive scale, or to dishonesty about one's achievements – it perhaps reflects something of a larger misconception concerning the nature of understanding itself. I believe it is rationalism's preoccupation with the public, the shared, and the rule-governed that lies at the heart of the problem. To try to demonstrate this, let us consider the following examples:

> I know that William the Conqueror invaded England in 1066, but I don't understand it.

> I know Darwin's book *The Origin of Species*, but I don't understand it.

> I've known Richard for years, but I've never really understood him.

I knew that living in an old house would be damp, cold, and inconvenient in many ways, but now (one winter later) I understand just what that means.

I knew that lung cancer and smoking are related, but until then (nursing a father suffering from cancer as a result of smoking) that didn't mean much to me.

She thought she knew what sadness was until she said goodbye to John.

How adequately does the rationalist account characterize the kind of understanding picked out in the second part of each statement?

Let us begin by acknowledging straight away that insofar as these statements refer to some kind of propositional knowledge, the rationalist account makes many important points about what it is to understand. Clearly one can have no understanding of a proposition unless one has some correct understanding of the public concepts in which it is framed. To take the first example, if one thought that William the Conqueror was a variety of Rhododendron, and 1066 the year before last, or worse, a telephone number, one has either a gross misunderstanding of the proposition, or, in the second case, no understanding at all – the statement becomes altogether unintelligible. This much, perhaps seems too obvious to be worth saying, but it does make absolutely clear the extent to which the role of the teacher in promoting a child's understanding must be concerned with helping him or her to internalize the correct – i.e. publicly agreed – meaning of terms.

But it also broaches another important issue for teaching: while there must be *some* correct understanding, it does not have to be *complete*. There is sometimes a tendency to suppose that one has to understand one thing fully before proceeding on to the next thing. This is clearly an error, and one which has no doubt led to a lot of boredom and frustration in situations where children have been cajoled into an endless series of repetitive exercises intended to give them a complete grasp of some 'vital' point thought to be essential to any further progress. This 'fallacy of learning through perfected steps', as Robert Dearden once called it, sets unnecessary obstacles to further learning, undermines the confidence and curiosity of those children whose learning is frequently stalled in this way, and quite misunderstands the way in which public concepts get their meaning.

One of the things that the games analogy makes clear is that concepts do not exist in isolation. They do not have discrete meanings that can be fully comprehended: they *depend upon each other for their meaning*. They exist in webs of interrelationship, and there is not necessarily one way into this web, nor one route through it, and there is rarely any pre-specifiable 'amount' of understanding of any one term in the web that must be achieved before *some* understanding of other terms in the web can be gained. In the same way that the meaning of the term 'goal' in football can only be understood in the context of some understanding of the game as a whole, so terms such as 'mother' and 'son' can only be understood through their relationship to a whole web of other terms such as 'father', 'daughter', 'sister', 'family', etc. which articulate a set of social relations and responsibilities. A developed understanding of any one of these implies some understanding of the others and thus from the point of view of the concepts themselves, it is no more easy, or more difficult, to begin with any particular one of them.

Similarly, in an area such as maths, frequently thought of as highly 'logical' and often conceived by teachers and authors of schemes as something to be developed through a linear progression of ideas, it is clear that, say, the term 'seven' is dependent upon the meaning of other numbers, the concept of number itself, the operations that can be performed upon them, and so forth, and that one gains in understanding of the 'sevenness' of seven as one explores this web of interrelationships. There is no one route to achieving this because, in truth, there is no such thing as *the* meaning of 'seven'. It has meanings, and these depend upon the context in which it is being used.

This aspect of more sophisticated rationalist accounts lends support to the view that, often, promoting understanding is not linear, but spiral, and that it is rarely to be achieved through one avenue only. I think that it is hard to overstress the importance of this for teaching, programmes of learning, and consequently for the teacher–pupil relationship as a whole. And it is a point whose importance is in severe danger of being overlooked by those who advocate any kind of national curriculum which seeks to impose detailed sequential sets of attainment targets during the process of education. Some characterization of the broad framework of goals that our education system should be working towards is perhaps beneficial in giving teachers a keener sense of direction than they have sometimes had and in ensuring a certain kind of equality of opportunity, but close pre-specification of learning objectives on anything but an individual basis is likely to be highly detrimental to the learners who are at the centre of the exercise. Such pre-specification ignores the myriad routes it is often possible to take through our complex webs of interrelated concepts, and infringes the freedom of individual children in negotiation with informed teachers to follow those paths which have most personal meaning.

Let us return now to our list of examples. Presumably it is further knowledge of this interlinking kind that would make good the lack of understanding claimed in the William the Conqueror example. Above and beyond the meaning of the terms, the speaker needs to relate this proposition to a web of others concerning ambitions and motives, and social and economic pressures. Similarly, to understand Darwin's book *The Origin of Species* would require a grasp of the fundamental concepts of evolutionary theory, and the evidence that Darwin marshals in its support. This all seems to fit fairly well with the rationalist view of understanding as linking things (e.g. concepts, pieces of information, evidence) together in accordance with publicly shared rules and standards. But does this hold good in the same way for the other examples?

In these examples one could suppose that the person knew the relevant facts, and that the facts were linked together in accordance with the relevant public concepts. The enlarged understanding was not so much a result of acquiring more of these linked facts, rather somehow the person concerned came to know these same things in a deeper way, i.e. understanding has, as it were, developed through qualitative deepening rather than quantitative addition. Thus, to take the 'living in an old house' example, the speaker may have known in a perfectly adequate way from the point of view of public meanings that a leaking roof leads to dampness, draughts and coldness in winter, but now in some more subjective sense this actually means more to him.

This is not, I think, simply to make the well-known point that understanding requires that new information and ideas become linked onto a person's existing understanding, beliefs, and previous experience. It is, no doubt important to be aware of understanding as having this subjective dimension, i.e. that we need to complement linking into the public network of shared concepts with a linking into an individual's existing personal framework of experiences. But such two-way linking remains essentially concerned with understanding through breadth, rather than depth, of relationship. The examples we are now considering seem to suggest something rather different. The occupant of the old house had already related concepts of cold and damp to his previous experience; in the smoking and lung cancer case the facts and their relationship all made perfectly good sense; Jane knew in a perfectly good way what sadness was before she said goodbye to John; but each of them now knows what they already knew in some further sense. What was formerly known in an averaged-off way has gained a felt personal cogency, such that the person's outlook has been significantly transformed. The meaning of what they knew has been 'brought home' to them, their understanding is such that they now really appreciate the *weight* of what they know. The origin and nature of this 'subjective weight' in understanding is one of the chief concerns of the next section of this book, but something of its importance is indicated by the following illustration taken from the writing of the nineteenth-century philosopher Søren Kierkegaard.

Kierkegaard: subjective depth of understanding

Kierkegaard was very much against what he regarded as the shallow understanding of deep things possessed by many of his post-Enlightenment contemporaries. In particular, he singled out their attitude to the Christian faith – their claims to have outgrown such faith and to have supplanted it with something superior, i.e. more rational. For Kierkegaard, these people who had claimed to have such understanding of faith that they could find it lacking and had now got beyond it, had no real conception of what faith is. He tries to illustrate this by considering their understanding of the story of Abraham and Isaac.[3]

We may recall that contrary to expectation, and though late in life, Abraham's great hope was realized: he had a son, Isaac. As Isaac grew up he became the thing that Abraham loved above all else in the world; for Abraham, Isaac was 'the best'. However, a day came when God required Abraham to take Isaac to Mount Moriah and sacrifice him as a burnt offering. And out of faith Abraham travelled for four days with his son at his side, went alone with him up the mountain, prepared for the sacrifice, drew his knife to strike, at which moment he saw the ram that God had prepared and knew that his son was to be spared. Now *there*, says Kierkegaard, was someone who knew faith, and what an awesome thing it is. He invites us to imagine the thoughts that must have been going through Abraham's mind as he journeyed beside his son, knowing what he was to do – with his own hands, for God was not going to do it for him. He would be responsible for it, do it of his own will (he could always turn back), and all for no reason that he could fathom. He would simply do it out of faith. Far from being something easily understood, such faith almost defies our imagination and if we began to understand it, would surely cause us to tremble.

Yet, many who in Kierkegaard's Denmark would know that story off by heart and claim to understand it, would barely be moved by it. 'Abraham was a great man: he was prepared to give to God the best' would be the sum of their understanding. How easy it is for such a summation to run off the tongue, and with such little distress as to hardly give pause for thought, and certainly not to impinge on the real business of getting on in life. Kierkegaard imagines a parson telling the story approvingly in a sermon, the parson himself hardly moved by it. He imagines members of the congregation listening comfortably to the story – one, perhaps casually stretches his legs, another finds a moment to tap out his pipe – as they hear again the story they all know and understand so well. He then imagines the following comi–tragic situation: one of the congregation, wishing to emulate Abraham's greatness, goes home and kills his own son.

> If the orator got to know of it, he perhaps went to him, he summoned all his clerical dignity, he shouted, 'O abominable man, off-scouring

89

of society, what devil possessed thee to want to murder thy son?' And the parson, who had not been conscious of warmth or perspiration in preaching about Abraham, is astonished at himself, at the earnest wrath which he thundered down upon that poor man. He was delighted with himself, for he had never spoken with such verve and unction. He said to himself and to his wife, 'I am an orator. What I lacked was the occasion. When I talked about Abraham on Sunday I did not feel moved in the least.' In case the same orator had a little superabundance of reason which might be lost, I think he would have lost it if the sinner were to say calmly and with dignity, 'That in fact was what you yourself preached on Sunday.' How could the parson be able to get into his head such a consequence? And yet it was so, and the mistake was merely that he didn't know what he was saying.[4]

Lacking an understanding of the awesomeness of the story he was telling, delivering it in a levelled-off and essentially uncomprehending manner, the parson had reduced Abraham's supreme act of faith into a cosy commonplace which any man might follow to his spiritual profit. His incapacity to feel and communicate the subjective weight of what he was saying and his inability to empathetically enter into the situation he described left him mouthing words both of whose real significance he had not the faintest notion, and whose simple reasoned meaning he was unable to accept, for in truth in his own mind they were completely worn out; he ran through them as a matter of form. Here, then, we seem to have a dimension of understanding that goes far beyond the idea of thought organized in accordance with public rules: a dimension of understanding which, if not overtly denied by rationalism (i.e. soft rationalism), is certainly not much illuminated by it, nor properly taken into account by it.

Yet, equally, may it not be thought from the example I have used that such understanding lies beyond the compass of education in the primary school? It is not altogether obvious that this is in fact the case. We are in part here considering the way in which one can, and sometimes should, be affected personally by what one knows. This capacity to understand through being affected, that is, through a form of passivity in which feeling comes unbidden and seems to constitute some more direct apprehension of a situation than calm rational scrutiny provides, is not only *not* beyond the experience of young children, *it is largely their natural way of experiencing things*. It is a way of under-standing, i.e. standing under the sway of, things that, largely under the influence of rationalism, we consistently tend to wean children away from, destroy their confidence in, and debase rather than develop and refine. By constantly demanding that their thoughts assume rational form and are backed up with rational justification we effectively communicate that rational standards set the standard for all thought. I would argue that understanding as 'standing under', or 'standing in the sway of' is of great importance across the primary school curriculum, representing, as it does, that dimension of understanding that is the true child of one of the most precious but perhaps most fragile motives for learning: a sense of wonderment.

In a time when so much emphasis is placed on learning for instrumental purposes and on understanding which is therefore shaped and restricted by those purposes, it may be of the greatest importance to keep open the door for a relationship to things which is not so restricted, but is more open and directly involved with things in the richness and depth of their possibilities. This is not to say that the affective response to things which I am taking to be a feature of young children's experience should simply be indulged. It is often, but not always, hopelessly self-centred and is capable of being as blindly obsessive as it is in some adults. Overweening jealousy, desire for power or material goods, are no more open to the richness of things than rigid pigeon-holing. It is rather to say that the capacity for affective involvement which has both a directness of contact with its object because it is felt, and openness to it because of its directness and fluidity, is something that needs to be cultivated in terms of its own possibilities for integrity, rather than forced to wear the mantle of rationalism. What the integrity of this kind of thinking might amount to, and what it might mean for the development of thinking and understanding in the curriculum, will be explored in the next Part. Before moving on to this, let us take stock of some of the main themes which have arisen so far.

Rationalism: some provisional conclusions

The rationalist accounts we have examined draw attention to many points of importance in an understanding of what is involved in developing children's thinking. They draw attention to the variety of rule-structured forms that thinking may take and the way in which some aspects of meaning arise from these structures themselves. They show how it is possible for a certain kind of objectivity to gain a foothold in thinking by reference to publicly shared standards and the richness of communication that this makes possible. Clearly there must be immense implications for primary teaching here. At the very least the need for some careful analysis of the salient facets of the various thought games presently available should be a matter of some urgency. What are the fundamental procedures and standards that constitute these activities? Can we identify certain key concepts and ideas which could be progressively developed in children's thinking? If we can, is there any hierarchy between them which would indicate an order in which learning must occur? Rationalism emphasizes a way in which we must understand this 'what' of teaching before we can sort out the 'how' of teaching.

But there are further questions. What of the underlying motivation of each game – what kind of project with regard to reality does it express and what is its educational worth? As against the attempt of Hirst's hard rationalism to provide a formal blanket justification for the place of any knowledge game in the curriculum, the claim of Bailey's soft rationalism to decide this issue by the criterion of the contribution a form of thought has made to the attempts of humankind to understand themselves in their relationship to the world, suggests an important consideration in evaluating the wealth of activities and material available from an educational standpoint. So, too, is his gesture towards recognition of the importance of the individual's own understanding of things that are learnt. But the question remains as to the adequacy of the conception of these things that rationalism enables. Would a curriculum and approach to teaching that was founded on the principles and understandings of rationalism alone properly develop children's thinking and understanding? Or do they risk, as I have suggested,

the development of fluency in the domain of conventional understanding at the cost of a certain poverty of subjective response –
the result of which could on occasion be gross misunderstanding?

NOTES AND REFERENCES

1 See Peters, 'Subjectivity and standards', reprinted in the collection
  Psychology and Ethical Development (1974). Here he quotes with approval
  G. H. Mead's idea that the reasonable man adopts the point of view of
  the 'generalized other'.
2 Bailey (1992), p. 135.
3 See Kierkegaard (1843).
4 Ibid.

Part Three
An Existentialist Perspective

CHAPTER 8

An Existentialist Backdrop to Thinking and Understanding

In the last part of the previous chapter I began to indicate some of the shortcomings of the rationalist perspective in its ambition to give an account of the whole of thinking. One of the main contentions voiced was its lack of appreciation of the importance of 'subjective weight' in a person's understanding and general mode of relating to things, and its consequent overlooking of the role played by a person's own motivations in the meanings they are able to achieve in their thinking. In this chapter I intend to explore these notions further, and their consequences for how we understand the development of children's thinking.

Perhaps the first thing that needs to be emphasized as we enter this area of concern is that such a consideration undermines any notion that thinking proper is a purely intellectual activity that can somehow go on in splendid isolation from the personal life of the thinker. On this view, a person thinks from out of the particular situations in which they find themselves, and this means that integral to a person's thought are the emotions, attitudes, dispositions and motives that constitute the way they experience these situations. In an important sense, thinking is a product of living, and not something that goes on alongside it on some 'pure' dimension untainted by an individual's subjective concerns. It is *not* the creation of 'the generalized other' as R. S. Peters characterized the stance of rationality, and its meaning and validity cannot be adequately thought of in the terms that such a characterization invites. We are forced therefore to look beyond the confines of public rules of thought to the quality of the conscious life of the thinker, if we are to properly understand thinking and its development. This is a central (and, for some, controversial) point, and it clearly demands a much broader perspective than rationalism has, at least traditionally, allowed. Candidates claiming to offer illumination on the quality of human life are of course many and varied, but as previously mentioned, I intend to look at the contribution of one such perspective, namely that of existentialism, loosely conceived.

Existentialism and the extent of human freedom

Existentialism is a rich vein of philosophical and literary thought which begins with the premise that 'existence precedes essence'. This places it in direct opposition to much of traditional metaphysics which is the legacy of Plato. Instead of supposing that thought has as its basic point of reference an underlying world of objective truths and essences which the operation of rationality can disclose to us, it claims that the starting point for thought is our involvement in a concrete world of particular things and situations in which we conduct our everyday business of living, and which is most directly revealed to us not by our intellect but by our present *mood*. That is to say, it is how we are in the world in which we find ourselves that constitutes the reality which is the touchstone of thought, not a set of pure abstract ideas or 'essences' which this world somehow inadequately reflects. Sheer existence comes first, and is the context in which all our interpretations of experience are embedded.

Having pointed out this common element, it would be wrong though to think of existentialism as a single homogeneous school of thought – any more than rationalism is. It represents rather a mood, a stance towards life, susceptible to many derivations; for example, there are theistic and atheistic versions. But one preoccupation which runs through much existentialist thinking is the nature and place of human freedom and its affect on how we think and understand the world. If thinking is embedded in concrete human existence, and freedom or the lack of it is an essential feature of this existence, then a fuller examination of this notion seems to be warranted. In what follows, I will draw particularly on the views of Martin Heidegger and Jean-Paul Sartre to illustrate this connection between thinking, understanding, and freedom, but first it is necessary to say a little more about the general character of existentialism in its attempt to illuminate our situation.[1]

The first point to emphasize is that in keeping with its tenet that existence precedes essence, existentialism does not attempt to produce abstract general, 'objective' principles to explain or guide human behaviour. Rather it focuses on the issue of how individuals confront the problem of their *own* existence – what they are to do with their life in the real situations in which they find themselves – and their possible attitudes towards this. It focuses, then, on the predicament of individuals in their unique lived situations, and in this sense embodies an anti-intellectual, anti-theoretical approach. Indeed, there is an important sense in which existentialism would regard, for example, a systematic morality with its assumptions of objective rightness and wrongness which can be encapsulated in a set of binding universal moral principles as something of a fraud, a form of self-deception.

For example, to suppose that somehow one's choice over a course of action is curtailed because moral principles demand it, and concomitantly to think that in this way the level of personal responsibility for what one does is reduced, would be to deceive oneself over the extent of one's essential freedom for the way one conducts one's life. In this particular case the existentialist would argue that we have no ultimate guarantees that we've got the right moral principles, therefore we have still as individuals to accept them, to choose whether to act upon them. And even if we accept certain principles in a general sense, we have still to decide *how* best to act upon them and to resolve possible conflicts between them. That is to say, general principles have still to be applied to the particular situations in which individuals find themselves, and there can be no complete, preordained, recipe for life. We must each make our own choices. Here we have an example of existentialism's sensitivity to, on the one hand, the uniqueness of each person and the situations he or she lives through, and on the other hand, the possibility of ignoring this uniqueness – of lapsing into essentially unthinking conformity to mass opinion and group norms and standards through apathetic obedience to social expectations and generalized application of principles irrespective of subtle nuances of each situation.[2]

Let me now explore this theme of freedom in a little more depth. For the existentialist, integral to the very idea of distinctively human being, as contrasted with the way of being of, say, things or animals, is a certain sort of freedom. Unlike animals and things, human beings are not wholly causally determined, *they could always have done other than they did.* Whether they consciously acknowledge it or not, they are always in a position of choice. What does this amount to precisely? I think Max Scheler caught part of the meaning of this when he once referred to man as the animal that can say 'No' to nature. He meant by this that humankind has the capacity not to act solely out of instinct and conditioned reflex. We need not automatically hit out when angry, grab food when hungry, be altruistic if this serves the survival of the species, etc. We can, as it were, say 'No' to such basic impulses. (Indeed, this is precisely what a growing baby has to learn to do.) Human beings can do this because they have the ability to stand back from the immediate situation and become an object for themselves: they have a capacity for *self-awareness*.

Self-awareness, then, is an idea that is essential to the notion of human being. Through acts of detachment from on-going events we can reflect upon our position in a particular situation – can reflect upon not only what *is* the case, but on what *could be* the case, that is to say, on the possibilities that are open to us. And once we do this we are unavoidably in a position of choice, like it or not! Every act of choice, then, involves detachment of oneself from the on-going world and reflection on possible alternatives. And every such act of detachment and reflection condemns one to having to choose. To do nothing is itself a choice.

To summarize, existentialism emphasizes the way in which human beings are agents in their own right: it is their essence not to be just passively carried along by events, by blind forces, like a dried leaf in the breeze, migrating lemmings, a herd of cattle. They can have purposes that they have chosen for themselves, and no matter what the objective situation, they always have this choice. There is always some room for them to choose.

But now, doesn't this emphasis on the pervasiveness of human freedom run counter to common experience? Aren't there all sorts of situations which we would not naturally characterize in terms of freedom? For example, consider a wartime situation of possibly saving one's comrades but at the probable expense of one's own life: either one could warn them of their danger or escape oneself. Here the range of options is severely restricted, and neither of them is particularly pleasant. But there remains an important sense in which one is still free: there is a choice to be made, and the harder and more serious the choice, the more valuable it may be. Sartre would say that it is in situations like these that one chooses *oneself* – the sort of person one is to be, say, hero or coward, and thus gives oneself meaning.

Or, to take another rather extreme situation, suppose one is told to do something at gunpoint – e.g. 'hand over the money'. It seems natural to say that one had no choice here, one was forced to do as one was told. But the existentialist would point out that even here there was a choice. We don't have to do what we are told to do at gunpoint. Suppose we were told to harm a young child; mightn't we then refuse, and risk the gun? This sort of point was recognized in the trials of Nazi concentration camp officers after World War II. Despite unpleasant, perhaps fatal, consequences of not obeying orders, they were accounted both responsible for what they did and blameworthy. The courts held not only that they could have done otherwise, but that they should have done so.

Inauthenticity: the denial of freedom and responsibility

The existentialist, then, argues that we are essentially free: no matter what the external situation there is always some room for choice as to how we will *respond* to it. However, he would readily agree that it does not always appear this way to us in our everyday experience; we are often not consciously aware of this freedom and do not use it. We tend to act automatically, and out of habit. Indeed, he would claim that if we survey human life in general, it is clear that for most of the time we try to hide this very fact of our existence from ourselves. For example, Heidegger claims that we 'flee in the face of the truth of our existence', our individual freedom. We deceive ourselves into thinking that we don't have this freedom. For most of the time we live 'inauthentically', or, as Sartre would put it, in 'bad faith'. Why, according to the existentialist, we should do this, I will go into presently. First, I would like to illustrate what existentialists have in mind when they talk of being inauthentic. Examples abound.

I will start with some fairly specific ones, and invite the reader to consult his or her own experience to judge their plausibility and the general characterization of human life that ensues. We deny our own freedom by:

Trying to get others to make our decisions for us: What do *you* think I should do?

Pretending things are beyond our control, for example by supposing that everything has been decided by 'them' where we don't take the trouble to see just who 'they' are, and what influence we might bring to bear if we were determined enough.

Convenient fatalism: I know people say that smoking is dangerous but I believe you go when you are Called, etc. (This could be a genuine and deeply held belief, but sometimes it is an excuse for not acting.)

Personality traits: I just *am* the sort of person who loses his temper, is inconsiderate, etc., as if this just has to be accepted as an immutable fact.

Allowing ourselves to be determined by social stereotypes: I'm artistic and therefore it's natural that I should be temperamental.

Pretending that problems, and therefore choices, don't exist through various forms of double-think. Sartre gives the example of a girl giving her hand to an amorous partner. She is enjoying the flirtation but doesn't want to face up to the decision that has to be made as he gets more adventurous. She tries to distance herself from the problem by pretending that her hand is somehow separate from her, not hers to withdraw.

These examples are but limited instances of what the existentialist sees as being a very general condition. The extent to which we try to deny our individual uniqueness and our individual freedom to choose and thus shape our own lives is held to be extremely pervasive. According to Heidegger we are constantly tempted into the way of the 'crowd'. For the most part we allow our lives to be ordered in great detail by what the anonymous 'they' say and think, and keep ourselves too busy with our on-going everyday affairs to realize this. We submerge ourselves in the world by living busily and unthinkingly according to the roles, stereotypes, expectations, with which the 'they' provide us, and thus measure ourselves according to standards that are not truly our own. We lose ourselves in hobbies, pastimes, intellectual pursuits, and we make sure that we don't give ourselves the opportunity to think genuinely about our own unique individual existence. Instead we get comfortably carried along in what is essentially just 'gossip' or 'hearsay', and fashion in one form or another.

To take the former, for Heidegger 'hearsay' refers to that frame of mind in which we hear things and just pass them on down the line, without really making them our own by testing their validity in terms of our own unique existence. We don't ask 'What does this really mean for me?', or even probe the grounds for believing it. We just hear it or read about it, and say it or write about it – as perhaps in casual conversation, or in an exam answer. In this frame of mind we live on the level of an essentially shallow and averaged-off collective understanding – what 'everybody' currently understands, such that problems that might throw us back on ourselves get glossed over by easy talk and groundless speculation. We tend, as it were, to talk and think largely in the third person.

In this way thinking is tranquillized, for such everyday understanding is never thrown into genuine puzzlement: it is all-knowing in the sense that it always has some ready-made answer up its sleeve to cover all possibilities. And the fact that, in truth, it is sometimes wrong doesn't put it out at all, for it is too busy with the next thing to acknowledge such faults. Think, for example, of the effects of a smear campaign: even if accusations are shown to be groundless something of the smear often sticks. In the gossip a web of unsubstantiated associations gets built up and these are tacitly carried forward while the truth gets quietly left behind, inconsistencies passing unremarked or submerged by the pressure of whatever is now current. In this way of living it's what the latest talk says of you, rather than what you are, that matters. It conditions what you think about yourself as well as what you think about others.

Now we should be clear here that in making reference to the idea of the 'they' when characterizing this frame of mind, Heidegger is not suggesting that there is some controlling group of other people. The 'they' *is an aspect of ourselves*. It characterizes a way of thinking that hides from us the possibility of having our own unique understanding of things, and thus allows us to escape facing up to our own unique possibilities and choices. Why should we try to escape from our individual freedom? The existentialist answer is simple: *because full consciousness of our freedom brings with it full consciousness of our responsibility*.

The existentialist holds that freedom and responsibility are inseparable: in acknowledging our freedom we are forced to face up to our own responsibility for all that we do. We can neither pass this off onto someone or something else, nor can someone or something else take it away from us. We are stuck with it. From the beginning we are thrown into a world not of our choosing: we did not choose to be born into the society and time that we were born into; we did not choose the physical attributes of the bodies in which we will live out our lives; things will happen over which we have precious little control, e.g. our plans may come to fruition or they may come to naught due to factors quite external to us. Tomorrow one of us may be dead because someone made a silly mistake when they were driving. Yet in the midst of all this arbitrariness, we are free to choose and are responsible for what we do. There is nothing behind us, as it were, that we can fall back on to make our choices for us, tell us what to do, nor is there some preordained objectively compelling ideal in the future towards which we must direct ourselves. At base, human existence is not reasonable, not rational, but *absurd*. We must make our choices and take responsibility for them in the face of this absurdity. It pervades all that we do.

It is interesting to note here that this was as true for the Christian existentialist, Søren Kierkegaard, as for atheistic existentialists such as Sartre. Kierkegaard held that Christian belief will never be something rationally or scientifically justifiable; if it were, it would no longer be a *religious* belief. Christian belief requires a leap of faith – and you are responsible for it. Someone who, say, turns to the life of Christ as a source of guidance is making a choice: they could have done otherwise. They remain responsible for all that they do in His name, or guided by His example.

Now clearly this account of human existence has important

consequences for the idea of helping children to develop as individuals: part of our long-term task would be to bring them gradually to an understanding of the nature, extent and significance of their freedom. But also, and very much to our present point, it has large implications for the quality of thinking in which we might be encouraging children to engage.

For example, it would alert us to questions concerning how much of what presently goes on in schools has the quality of what Heidegger terms 'hearsay': how much is passed on to children in ways that do *not* invite them to evaluate what they have learnt in their own terms, and thus make it their own? John Holt[3] and others have claimed that there are tremendous pressures on children in school to set aside what they really think in order the better to produce what they believe their teacher wants, or will keep them 'in' with their peer group. In this situation, even the rebels rarely truly express themselves, but rather engage in a parallel form of 'counter-hearsay'.

One would need to ask, then, is the time required to explore personal attitudes to what is learnt too rarely given? If so, on this view, what is learnt is likely to remain lodged in the mind as so much information which will be applied in a manner largely determined by others and therefore with a diminished sense of personal responsibility. As such it is, therefore, only very partially understood, lacking the personal significance which would lift it above the level of what is simply current and 'known', or 'knowable', by all. It remains thought in an averaged-off way, sustained in a way of thinking – a mind – which is essentially owned by the 'they'. For the existentialist, to reinforce this already pervasive frame of mind would be a charade of developing children's thinking and a denial of their potential for becoming truly responsible individuals. It would leave them perhaps knowledgeable, but bereft of réal meaning and personal integrity – their thinking essentially mimicking that of others.

Authenticity

How, then, is the potentially vicious circle of inauthenticity and enmeshment in the 'they' to be broken? For the present, let us return to the general, as against the school, context. To be shown the truth of one's situation, and to be encouraged to discuss and reflect upon the significance of what one learns is a start, but simply stated thus, has its dangers. A purely intellectual acknowledgement is not enough, and, like anything else, one might simply relate to it at the level of hearsay and fashion. (In this respect one might recall the trendy existentialist rebels of the 1940s and 1950s.) How does one achieve the deeper level of response that authenticity requires? For understanding that is properly grounded in the existence of an individual, an element of opportunism may often be involved.

Sometimes something just happens that throws us back upon ourselves and makes us withdraw from the crowd for a while. Perhaps some long-cherished project suddenly collapses (or on the other hand suddenly becomes a real possibility). Perhaps one learns of the death of a close friend or relative, witnesses a fatal accident, or has a narrow escape oneself. Such experiences can cut the familiar everyday ground from under one and impart a slightly different, strange, aspect to things. In this way we may be brought to a mood in which the crowd can have nothing to say to us, and we see the on-going gossip and fashion for what it is; our comfortable and reassuring absorption in the everyday is disturbed for a short time.

It is at moments like these, then, that we may begin to come to ourselves, to seriously reflect upon the meaning of our own existence and what we really value in life. According to Heidegger, in this mood we can truly hear the call of our own conscience, and can be brought up against the one immutable fact of our life: our own death. We now confront this not in terms of idle speculation as to how or where we might die, but rather as a full conscious acknowledgement of the force of the fact that each of us *will* die. This, Heidegger holds, gives us a proper perspective from which to view our lives. And, however the 'they' might view it, this concern with death is not to be dismissed as a morbid fetish. On the contrary, a genuine awareness of our own death individualizes us because it forces us as individuals to face up to the problem of what we are going to do with our lives.

On Heidegger's account, then, the essence of human being is not so much that we are rational, symbol users, etc. (though we are these things to a greater or lesser extent), but that we are *mortal*, meaning by this that we live in an awareness of the fact that we ourselves will die – though we usually try to cover this awareness over. And the real problem for each of us then, the problem that provides the context for all our choices and understanding, is not what is the meaning of life where we look outside ourselves (e.g. to religion or science) for the answer; it is: *what meaning will I give to my life*? What will I hold true to in the light of the fact that I will surely die? This is held to be individualizing because it is a question each person must answer for him or herself.

Now it may seem at this point that all this is getting to be a far cry from children in the primary school. Surely, it may be argued, issues to do with our mortality and the meaning we give to our lives are matters for mature reflection by adults. Even if we were to concede that it might form a long-term aim of some general notion of education conceived as personal growth, to attempt to introduce such issues to young children would be both beyond their understanding and a source of unnecessary anxiety to them. A response to such objections, and some consequences for what it is to develop children's thinking and understanding in the primary school, is the subject of the next chapter.

NOTES AND REFERENCES

1 In particular, I will be drawing upon ideas expressed in Sartre's *Being and Nothingness* (1943), especially Part I, Ch. 2, and Heidegger's *Being and Time* (1927), especially Sections 26–27 and 35–37. An interesting critique which raises important issues concerning some aspects of Heidegger's thinking can be found in Adorno (1986).

2 With regard to the latter, history is littered with examples of the destructive effects of those who have had a strong sense of the 'Moral Law' and a weak sense of human compassion which would have allowed them to temper their high principles so as properly to meet differing circumstances. Ibsen's play *Brand* is a particularly powerful exemplification of this in literature: Brand, the village priest who, through his stern will and uncompromising adherence to his principles, brings about the death of both his wife and child, alienates himself from his people who come to revile him, and who, as he is engulfed by the death he has brought upon himself, recognizes the cold emptiness of his life and cries in despair: 'Answer me, God, in the moment of death! If not by will, how shall Man be redeemed?' And a voice replies: 'He is the God of love.'

3 Holt (1990).

CHAPTER 9
Self-Expression in Learning

A résumé

In the previous chapter I tried to make the general point that the development of thinking is a facet of mind, and that therefore the quality of such development is closely related to the quality of the conscious life of the individual mind which sustains it. Thus in wishing to understand the factors which constitute the development of thinking we must look not only at whatever logical structure there may be to the concepts being learnt – their public meaning – but also the subjective structure of the individual mind which is to receive these concepts. If this is so, it is clear that an important feature of this element is not simply its existing cognitive structure (an aspect much laboured by psychologists such as Piaget) but its affective structure: its stance towards what is being learnt in particular, and its attitude towards the world in general. These will be important elements in determining the 'subjective weight' of what a person knows.

Thus, we must be alert to the different modes in which consciousness relates to things and the motivations that underlie these if we are to appreciate the way in which what a child learns is affecting the sense of an organic life referred to in Chapter 1. Our brief exploration of existentialism highlighted two such broad modes: the authentic and the inauthentic, and I have tried to sketch in a preliminary way some of the far-reaching consequences of these two modes for an understanding of the development of thinking. However, the question was raised as to how relevant this can be to teaching children of the primary school age. I shall now attempt to relate what I have taken to be some of the insights of existentialism to the development of children's thinking in the primary school. To bring home the importance of these considerations I intend to refer to an educational philosophy which is no doubt more familiar to many primary teachers than existentialism: the philosophy of child-centredness.

Child-centredness and authentic self-expression

Child-centred approaches to education have now a long, if somewhat chequered, history which goes back some two hundred years or so to Rousseau.[1] While during this period it has taken a variety of specific forms, and undergone various transformations, one enduring tenet lies at its kernel: the idea that *real learning involves the self-expression of the learner*. That is to say, it makes a fundamental claim that while children may be brought to acquire all sorts of facts and skills through a process in which they are essentially treated as passive receivers, for them to achieve a proper understanding of what can be so acquired they need to relate it all to their own experiences, concerns, and purposes. Thus they need to be personally active in their learning – to express themselves in it – for understanding to occur, for it is held that understanding is not something which can be simply implanted from outside, it has to be constructed by the individual, and this requires that they are given the opportunity to pursue it in their own way.

From this basic assumption many things seemed to follow. There arose the notion that the curriculum should be based on children's current interests, and that they should have significant freedom of choice with regard to the direction their learning would take. This in turn led to a whole gamut of recommendations as to how education should be organized: individualized learning; small group work; the integrated day; project work; learning through play, discovery and discussion; practical experimentation; open-plan buildings; using the environment as an important resource, etc. Perhaps most important of all were the seeming implications for the role of the teacher. On the child-centred model the teacher was required to relinquish the role of ultimate authority on what, when, how, and where things were to be learnt, and became more of a facilitator in children's efforts to pursue their own interests. This became interpreted by some as a role of such passivity that it consisted in little more than that of keeping some sort of general order in the classroom.

But, let us now bring to these issues some of the considerations that I have drawn from existentialism. Firstly, let us look more carefully at the notion of self-expression which I have suggested lies at the heart of this whole approach to education. I would like to suggest that the existentialist perspective can help to clear away some common misunderstandings of this notion which have led sometimes to its rejection as an educational consideration, and sometimes to educational malpractice.

To begin with, the idea that children will achieve self-expression if allowed almost total freedom to do what they like would clearly be a nonsense on this view. In truth, authentic self-expression is far more likely to be criticized for its austerity than because it is laissez-faire. Self-expression cannot be simply a matter of 'doing one's own thing' regardless of the consequences: authentic self-expression must involve acknowledging that one is the author of one's actions, and it is this sense of personal responsibility that gives them their feeling of meaningfulness, a feeling that is lacking if one is simply carrying out someone else's instructions, or complying with what is commonly expected. To deny responsibility for the consequences of one's actions both for oneself, and for others, is precisely to deny that those actions were really one's own. Self-expression, then, is not to be equated with unthinking spontaneity or unbridled ego-centrism.

Related to this, existentialism also makes it clear that neither is self-expression just a matter of doing what one normally or habitually does. One may not normally *be* very self-expressive in the authentic sense of this term: rather one may normally be caught up in the previously-described strategies of self-deception, unthinking conformity to social and peer group expectations, and the superficiality of 'hearsay', such that awareness of personal choice and responsibility is minimal or altogether absent. Certainly many children will be liable to act and think in ways that simply reflect what happens to be currently popular, or dominant characters in the class or at home, and to generally prefer the security of going along with the rest of the group. Further, it would be false to assume that all, or indeed very many children, will necessarily relish opportunities to exercise what powers they may have for positive initiative, independence, choice and personal responsibility – even over matters like when to sharpen a pencil! Indeed, some, at least, seem content to be told in minute detail what to do and can show signs of withdrawal or resentment when this is not forthcoming. For them the need for attention, or feelings of insecurity or apathy might provide stronger motives.

Finally, self-expression should not be equated (as it sometimes is) with being extroverted, 'emotional' or 'loud' – always ready with an opinion, always busy, active, and generally 'prominent'. Keeping silence, being thoughtful and reflective, are often more truly self-expressive. Indeed, the person with everything 'up front' can be a parody of self-expression, such behaviour being more a substitute for having little depth of personal development. Clearly, then, and at the very least, a classroom in which children are encouraged to be self-expressive will not correspond to the popular caricature of a room full of noise and blustering 'busyness'. Further – and this is very important – self-expression becomes viewed very much as something to be *achieved* rather than as something that will just naturally 'happen' if we allow it.

All this ties in closely with the earlier point, that the development of thinking is more than simply a matter of cognitive development. Quality of thinking and understanding inevitably involves dispositions: to be honest, responsible, open, and reflective. It will also be true that if real learning involves such self-expression it will carry with it an element of personal risk and therefore require a sense of self-worth sufficient to cope with this. To understand how this is so, we need to explore more fully the way in which self-expression relates to understanding, by pressing the question: How is it that things can come to have personal meaning ('subjective weight')?

In the discussion of 'hearsay' in the previous chapter, it was suggested that things acquire subjective weight through the responsible placing of value on them. But in terms of what, can we value things? It would seem that the answer to this must be: the things that bring us into personal contact with the world in the first place – our personal (i.e. authentic) concerns. It is these which allow things to matter to us and enable us to enter into a personally meaningful relationship with the world because it is only by expressing them and feeling the world's response (either actually, or through acts of imagination) that we can feel what our thoughts really mean. This is our means of growing both in knowledge of the world, and in self-knowledge, for it is in this interplay that we learn the consequences of our thoughts, attitudes and beliefs, and thus allow them to be refined and enlarged.

For example, we will understand a situation as friendly – and in such and such a way – to the extent that the expression of our genuine concern for friendship receives a positive response; an idea is illuminating to the extent that it satisfies our genuine concern to understand something; that the next train leaves in ten minutes matters to us to the extent that we are genuinely concerned to catch it. In other words, precisely how and why things matter to us personally – our own evaluation and understanding of them – is a reflection of our genuine concerns, either already present, or evoked by the situation itself. Learning through such self-expression, then, is 'real' in a double sense: it has personal cogency, and it is 'realistic' through its constant reference to the real world of things, people and institutions. Our concerns are, as it were, our personal bridge into that world.

To return now to the issue of personal risk: it is important to recognize how much such learning involves a personal investment, a certain giving of oneself. In much the same way that a novel comes to life – is properly 'read' – only when the reader lends his or her life to the characters – in some sense lives their experiences and situations with and for them, feeling their hopes and fears, etc., so the learner must give him or herself over to the encounter with what is to be learnt, giving it life by being prepared to go with it and personally accept what it brings. In opening oneself up in this way one becomes vulnerable, for failure will matter personally, leaving one in mid-air, confused, at a loss, etc.; and such an upshot is as likely as rapid success and satisfaction.

Further, in being willing to be personally affected by one's learning, facets of one's own identity may be brought into question – hitherto firmly held beliefs and attitudes being disturbed. Indeed, there is an important sense in which our personal identity largely *consists in* our beliefs, attitudes, and concerns, and is therefore always to some degree at stake in real learning.[2] It is for this reason that educational learning has rightly been characterized as concerned with the personal growth of the individual –

a point perhaps partially recognized by the National Curriculum proposal for aspects of what has been termed 'personal and social education' to be an important element in its cross-curricular dimensions and themes.

Clearly all this suggests that far from diminishing the role of the teacher in education, attention to authentic self-expression in children's learning and the quality of subjective weight in their thinking and understanding places great demands on it. The sensitivity and acumen required of the teacher in creating conditions conducive to such learning could hardly be overemphasized. I shall spell out in more detail what this might entail.

The role of the teacher in promoting real learning

I will begin by reiterating a fundamental point that existentialism makes about authentic self-expression: we cannot expect it simply to develop in children by itself, if only we'd 'let' it. The attitudes that lie at its kernel are highly dependent on the social environment in which children grow up. The attitudes that I have in mind here are ones such as a sense of self-worth, having the courage of one's convictions, tenacity in the face of adversity, confidence to question, take risks, face consequences, be constructively self-critical. These are all essential if children are to genuinely engage in thinking and construct their own understanding of things in such a way as to endow them with subjective weight. And engendering them will call for great skill and involvement on the part of the teacher. To suppose that one can simply provide 'a stimulating environment' and then sit on the sidelines would indeed be an abrogation of the teacher's responsibilities, and would be based on a misconception as to how it is possible for children's thinking to develop. It is undoubtedly true that children can and do learn a great deal by themselves without the direct guidance of adults. We must respect this. But equally, it is the case that there are limits and obstacles which it is unlikely or impossible for them to surmount without the aid of a caring adult.

We have previously noted (in Chapter 4) that from the purely cognitive point of view, it is hard to see how children can acquire by themselves, through the use of their senses, many important concepts because of abstract elements to them. We can now add that from the affective point of view, while young children may have many positive attitudes deriving from their relative innocence and a degree of natural curiosity, mixed with these, and sometimes very prominent, will be others such as timidity, apathy, insecurity, hostility, boredom, complacency, superiority/ inferiority, which can in varying degrees get in the way of authentic learning. Thus the teacher has a very active role to play in encouraging and supporting children; in provoking, questioning, suggesting possibilities. That is to say, teaching on this view becomes an *empathetic challenging*[3] of children to come to terms with, and extend, their own thoughts and feelings, and to create an ethos of mutual respect in which this can occur in a non-threatening way for both pupils and teacher!

This view, then, demands a balance between a respect for the thinking that children are presently engaged in, and a feel for the possibilities for its refinement and enlargement. And it places at the centre of such development, not simply the structure of public disciplines of thought in terms of which rationalism sees the mind of the child is to become patterned, but the *quality of the teacher–pupil relationship*. If learning which arises out of authentic self-expression, i.e. expression that gets below immediate and superficial wants and interests (which are sometimes a cover or substitute for deeper concerns and anxieties) is to be fostered, then teachers must be prepared to enter a relationship of empathetic openness and responsiveness with their pupils. When this happens we are likely to have confirmed for us what we already know but too rarely properly acknowledge in terms of its centrality to education, namely that children are real people and that like real people, they often have deep-seated concerns about themselves and the world. For example, they can have worries about illness and death (a project on 'Health' with 9-year-olds in which I was once involved revealed that several children suffered from a long-standing fear of dying from cancer and, indeed, the prospect of death itself), about personal relationships and their breakdown, as well as those more conventional 'childish' concerns which we find it less threatening to allow them to express. These can all be normal, healthy, *real* concerns and we do a child no service if we turn some into dark spectres haunting the edge of consciousness. Indeed, on the view we are now considering, the child's growth as a whole person precisely consists in their being honestly explored and better understood. Such deeper concerns become central to, rather than peripheral to, his or her education.

It becomes a vital role of the teacher, then, to help children to articulate their concerns without overbearing fear of censure; to formulate their ideas and responses, and to indicate possible ways forward. In this context, the vast resources of culture (itself a response to the whole gamut of human concerns and dilemmas) from fairy tales to philosophy[4] – can be drawn upon, but at need, i.e *as and when they are felt to have a contribution to make to the child's own understanding*, rather than being turned into a sterile strait-jacket of pre-specified teaching objectives. For teachers to be able to facilitate this, they will clearly need to have a sense of the vitality of culture themselves. This requirement has wide implications for their own education.

In a later chapter on structuring children's learning, I will attempt to spell out in more detail some specific points that these considerations suggest for the activities of teaching. But at this juncture let me summarize a general claim that is being made by saying that we must beware underestimating the degree of seriousness that children are capable of, and the possibility that in their own ways and at their own levels their thinking and understanding is as much a response to the problems and dilemmas of the human condition as is that of adults, and is equally subject to the pressures and counter-pressures that the notion of authenticity draws to our attention. Advocates of the existentialist perspective count it as one of its great strengths that it challenges us to see education, at whatever stage, as contributing to initiation into what it is to lead a human life, and not as something hived off from the rest of a child's existence. This applies both 'horizontally' in terms of the child's existence outside school, and 'vertically' in terms of a past and an open future which holds possibilities wider and deeper than those encompassed by intellectual and career success, or contribution to economic growth. It reminds us to bear in mind that any education worthy of the name should contribute to equipping people to eventually take up the risk of their own lives and decide for themselves what they are to do with it, and what meaning to give it.[5]

A reservation

This examination of an existentialist perspective on the development of thinking and understanding has highlighted the claim
that freedom and responsibility give subjective weight to learning,
and thus make it 'real'. On this view great emphasis is placed
on respecting the uniqueness of the individual and the role of the
teacher in supporting this wherever it may lead. While such an
approach clearly throws up many pressing organizational and
resource difficulties (which will be addressed in Part Four), might
it not also be criticized at the level of principle on the grounds
that it will encourage thinking which is unacceptably self-centred,
and perhaps insufficiently in touch with the social basis of thought
and knowledge?

It might be thought at this point that there is an obvious way
forward. Why not simply combine the subjective dimensions of
thinking highlighted by the notion of authenticity with the
social/objective dimensions emphasized by rationality? In this
way could we not have the virtues of both and arrive at a more
adequate account of what it is to develop children's thinking and
understanding? No doubt there is much to be said for this –
though we would have to be clear about exactly what we meant
by it. To accommodate the demands of authentic learning it
would be necessary for the bodies of rational procedures and
knowledge to be drawn upon as a response to the requirements
of a child engaged in exploring his or her own concerns. As they
are incorporated into this activity, they will of course play a role
in restructuring it, but the seminal point is that things are viewed
this way round: it is the context of the individual child's concerns,
rather than the structure of public forms of knowledge viewed
independently of this, that sets the agenda for learning. Teaching
the public forms of knowledge in the context of respecting and
eliciting children's authenticity would aspire to developing an
understanding which is both rational and truly their own because
it has become an integral part of their individual self-expression.
We would then be aiming at a form of thinking which we might
term 'authentic–rational'.

Can we now suppose that in this way we would bring into
harmony the main dimensions of thinking, the subjective and the

objective? I think this would be premature. There are some pressing objections that, when pursued, indicate a further dimension of thinking and its development which is in increasing danger of being, if not entirely overlooked, seriously undervalued and distorted. I intend to explore this possibility in the next two chapters by examining some further facets of the issue of 'self-centredness'.

NOTES AND REFERENCES

1 Rousseau's *Emile*, first published in 1762, is often thought of as founding the child-centred tradition.

2 See, for example, the notion of 'constitutive self' in Bonnett (1978).

3 I have tried to develop this idea in 'Personal authenticity and public standards', in Cooper (1986). It will also be taken further in Chapter 14. But see also the moving account given by Virginia Axline in *Dibs: In Search of Self* (1966) of what was involved in restoring a sense of self-worth and the capacity to become authentically self-expressive to a young child who was seriously repressed.

4 An interesting account of the contribution that fairy tales can make to a child's understanding of, and ability to come to terms with, his or her own concerns and anxieties is given in B. Bettelheim, *The Uses of Enchantment* (1976). Those who are sceptical about the ability of children in the primary age range to engage in and benefit from philosophical thinking might like to read G. Matthews, *Philosophy and the Young Child* (1980). They may also like to look at the materials produced by Karen Murris in *Teaching Philosophy with Picture Books* (1992).

5 It should be acknowledged here that such an educational aspiration is not completely ignored by rationalists. Indeed, in a certain sense, it could be thought to be amply illustrated by, for example, John White, who has placed much emphasis on the role of education in developing autonomy and the notion of considering different 'ways of life' and constructing 'life-plans'. Nonetheless the spirit in which this is undertaken bears all the hallmarks of rationalistic approaches (naturally enough!), thus transforming the aspiration into something rather different from the existentialist ideal.

CHAPTER 10

Authentic–Rational Thinking

Throughout the account that I gave of existentialism, ran the theme that freedom brings with it responsibility. In the sense that this implies acknowledging that one's actions have consequences, and that one is responsible for these, a certain amount of de-centring is clearly involved. But is this sufficient to meet the objection that developing authentic thinking will lead to self-centredness? Well, it is not altogether clear that it is, for might one not accept such responsibility and yet still think and behave selfishly? One might recognize unpleasant consequences for others and not care, or only care if this in turn is likely to have unpleasant consequences for oneself. In other words one could be authentically immoral. Now, this is clearly a serious deficiency in an account of what it is to develop children's thinking and is a further illustration of the way in which the whole issue is highly value-laden; not simply a matter of the development of a neutral intellect, but of motives and attitudes. Clearly then, and at the very least, an awareness of what is morally acceptable must be set alongside a concern for what is required for authenticity.[1]

But there are other important ways in which the self-centred objection may be pressed. One is as follows: mightn't authentic thinking (including now authentic–rational thinking) take very narrow channels for children whose concerns turn out to be very limited, and thus remain oblivious to that breadth of understanding which is sometimes taken as the mark of an educated person? Further, just how far are we to take the idea that understanding is something the individual constructs for him or herself? Surely most of what we learn has its origins from outside ourselves: we do not, and cannot, invent it all for ourselves – a point heavily stressed by the rationalists we considered in Part Two (see particularly Chapter 5).

In responding to objections of this kind, I think it is useful to make a distinction between self-centredness, and what I will term *self-referencing.* Self-centredness implies that one places oneself at the centre of all that is important, taking no real account of anything which lies beyond one's present desires and interests, and perceptions of what will serve one's own welfare. By contrast, self-referencing refers to a determination to understand what one learns in terms of one's own experiences, and to act in accordance with one's own beliefs and commitments. Self-referencing acknowledges that one is a member of a culture, that there are duties and obligations, that there is a vast stock of knowledge and understanding to inherit and discover. It simply represents an aspiration to make this truly one's own by relating to it dynamically, i.e. self-expressively. It requires that each individual is, in some significant sense, the *originator* of her judgements concerning the meaning and value of what she is learning. This is the fundamental tenet of personal authenticity in learning. I would now like to say a little more about it.

Self-referencing and the appropriation of thought[2]

Clearly the world of human meanings to which we wish to introduce the child exists quite independently of any individual child, and he or she has had no part in its creation. Without language there may be very little worthy of the name thought, and all of the situations and dilemmas a child finds him or herself in occur within the context of a pre-existing culture and are structured by it. Dilemmas over, say, who to play with, conflicting loyalties or duties, how to develop a new friendship or spend pocket money, are possible only against the backcloth of a set of inherited social situations and meanings. So talk of self-origination of thought clearly cannot be taken to mean that a child has somehow to invent all that he thinks for himself. Rather it expresses the demand that a child attempts to make what previously existed simply externally to him, his own. The issue is that of the appropriation of culture as against its passive acquisition or repressive transmission. And how do we make a fact or idea, or some other aspect of culture our own in this sense? The argument of the last two chapters has been that we do this by setting it in the context of our previous understanding, critically evaluating it, playing and experimenting with it,

119

deciding on our stance towards it in terms of the things that matter to us in our own existence, and accepting personal responsibility for the consequences of whatever stance we adopt.

Now this is clearly often likely to be a lengthy and on-going process which frequently will never be fully completed or finally resolved – our current understanding and commitment often having a highly provisional status. Yet to the extent that we go through this self-referencing process we truly internalize what was once external to us and become the originators or authors of our own thinking, as against merely reflecting the thoughts of others. And to the extent that we have assimilated and used public forms of thought in this process we would have achieved authentic-rational thinking. Not that thinking could ever *not* involve social meanings to a high degree, as our examination of the rationalist position has shown. It remains unclear, however, as to how far this point, of itself, need imply the intellectual disciplines in the way that, say, Hirst, and perhaps Bailey, assume.[3]

But now two further questions arise: firstly, can we really expect children of primary age to engage in such a demanding process of appropriation? And, secondly, is it appropriate to think that this degree of appropriation is necessary for everything that they may need to learn?

The answer to the first question is that the acquisition of this kind of understanding is always going to be a matter of degree, but to pursue it as far as one can – and at whatever level one can – is both to achieve the best understanding of which one is capable at the time, and at the same time to develop one's capacity for *future* understanding. By this latter I mean two things. Firstly, there is the point stressed in Chapter 9, and elsewhere, that quality of future understanding will depend upon the quality of that existing understanding with which it is to be integrated. A child whose current understanding of an area is, say, largely mechanical is likely to achieve a very different kind of grasp of further material to the child for whom the issues are *felt*. Secondly, I refer to the on-going enhancement of one's ability to engage fully with whatever one is learning through developing more demanding expectations and attitudes towards new experience. That is to say, authentic understanding is not so much the acquisition of various items such as sets of concepts, procedures and truth tests, as of an *outlook – a way of being*. As such, it will hugely affect the sorts of, and the quality of, situations one is likely to provide for oneself in the future. The child who has grown confident in asking questions, critically evaluating evidence from her own perspective and reflecting on the significance of what she has learnt, has a very different attitude towards life compared to the child who basically seeks accepted answers. She also makes very different demands upon her education and will tend to direct herself towards, and to create, different kinds of experience within it. In these related ways, then, the quality of a child's learning is largely a function of what that child brings to his or her learning – their present mode of thinking which conditions their interpretation of what they encounter and the depth of their engagement. As human beings, we exist understandingly. For the sake of quality of understanding in the future, as well as in the present, then, it is important to encourage the self-referencing mode.

Of course different children will differ in their aptitude and progress with regard to the self-referencing of thought. As achievement here is not simply a matter of cognitive ability, individual temperament and attitudes deriving from varying home backgrounds and cultures will influence the disposition of children to engage in such thinking. But this accepted, it is surely important that all children should at least be set on their way towards authentic understanding, and that we do not attempt to quickly prejudge how far they may get if they are given time, encouragement, and appropriate support. The point has previously been made that all children have personal concerns, however fluctuating and inadequately articulated they may sometimes be, in terms of which they can relate to and begin to evaluate what they learn. If this is so, the chief question is not whether children can make progress in this direction, but whether we as teachers think it worth the time and effort to develop it in the face of other pressures (such as feeling we have to 'cover the ground' – as determined, say, by a national curriculum, or other guidelines, devised independently of the particular children we are teaching).

Further, there is evidence to suggest that quite young children can engage in a surprisingly full way with important basic issues about human life, and that they can do it with a lack of prejudice and freshness that many adults find hard to achieve. Quite a startling illustration of this is cited by Gareth Matthews:

> Ian (six years) found to his chagrin that the three children of his parents' friends monopolized the television; they kept him from watching his favourite program. 'Mother,' he asked in frustration, 'why is it better for three people to be selfish than for one?'[4]

It is perhaps understandable that the mother was left non-plussed by this interesting question. Here the basic tenet of utilitarianism, the ethical theory which holds that we should endeavour to act so as to promote the happiness of the majority (and which it often seems natural to allow to guide our actions), is turned on its head, and one of its great defects – that it can be seen as an appeal to selfish motives that could result in the tyranny of minorities – is revealed. It is not of course being suggested that examples such as these (and Matthews provides a good number) show that children are consciously evaluating philosophical theories, but that their thinking can be sensitive to, and display some very telling reasoning with regard to issues which are the subject of such theories and which are basic to human life. There would seem to be something decidedly anti-educational about a system that intentionally or otherwise spurned such potential.

The second question concerning the appropriateness of aiming at a high degree of self-referencing in some areas of learning is an interesting one. In response, it is probably not possible to generalize very far, except to say that while it would be both unnecessary and impossible for *all* a person's understanding to have this element of inwardness, for which parts it should be sought and which not, must in large part depend upon those concerns which are central to a particular individual.

There are doubtless countless everyday things of which an individual needs only a token or working understanding in order to get by and be able to devote himself to those things which are, or should be, of more fundamental personal significance to him. For example, it is not at all clear why every child should develop an authentic understanding of, say, number bonds. It may be sufficient for him or her to be able to operate them in the everyday contexts in which they are useful without them acquiring a deep personal significance. Similarly, there may be other things of which it seems odd to suppose this kind of dimension is even intelligible, under normal circumstances, e.g. understanding certain basic rules of sentence construction or conventions involved in writing a letter, or using an index. These are simply important conventions that a child needs to be able to use. An element of authenticity remains desirable in that he needs to see the point of learning them, i.e. how they are useful to *him*, but their point is not itself of the kind that illuminates human experience.

On the other hand, there would seem to be many things which one cannot be said to understand at all properly if this element of broader personal significance is absent. For example, one could have a near perfect intellectual or technical grasp of the theory of evolution, or statistics on lung cancer or AIDS, the beliefs and achievements of one's own and other cultures, important historical and fictional characters and situations, but if this in no way affected one's outlook on certain aspects of life, one's understanding would be seriously deficient and would have contributed nothing towards one's personal growth. To take a specific, and I suppose now quite well worked, example, one could acquire all sorts of facts and figures about World War I, but to remain essentially unaffected by this knowledge, to have received it in a way that left one unmoved by the conditions under which this war was fought, the scale and pointlessness of the suffering and loss of life, would be grossly mis-educative. It is not simply that, as A. N. Whitehead once put it, 'A merely well informed man is the most useless bore on God's earth' (notwithstanding the fact that he'd doubtless do well on *Brain of Britain* or *Mastermind*), it is that such learning will not have *educated* one, for the significance of knowledge of this kind lies precisely in what it implies for our conception of our human situation and the course of our actions.

Thus while there may be a large number of things for which, because of their limited importance in a life, a relatively superficial and depersonalized understanding is sufficient, there are also many things that are frequently taught in this way, but which are shorn of their educational worth if they lack subjective weight. This idea has been forcefully expressed by Kierkegaard in the following way:

> I should suppose that education was the curriculum one had to run
> through in order to catch up with oneself, and he who will not pass
> through this curriculum is helped very little by the fact that he was
> born in the most enlightened age.[5]

The point here is that accumulation of more and more public
knowledge of itself does nothing to further our understanding. In
many ways we already 'know' too much, and our impressive
stock of knowledge sometimes beguiles us into thinking that if
only we had more of the same kind we could solve all our problems. But what we more often desperately need to do (both as
individuals and as a people) is to 'catch up' with what we already
know, and attempt to think through what it means, to us as
individuals, and for human being as a whole.

Perhaps this need is surfacing more frequently as rapid
technological advances in fields such as genetic engineering and
medicine open up possibilities and issues of which our grand-
parents could hardly have dreamed and with which our children
will increasingly have to deal. But, of course, the underlying
argument here is that currently prominent examples like these are
but the tip of the iceberg. Many of the everyday things which we
'know' and simply take for granted as 'well-known' or 'commonsense', can, on further reflection, display dimensions whose
significance had previously not touched us. The deeper meanings
in personal and human terms of the kinds of knowledge, the
achievements and the aspirations we currently value, and the
technologies, lifestyles, roles and relationships, that we allow
ourselves to become locked into – an honest personal apprehension of such things is essential if we are to grasp the true
significance of what we already in some sense know and do, and
thus regain true authorship of our lives.

Depth versus breadth of understanding

This last point really leads into the third aspect of the criticism
that authentic thinking will lead to self-centredness: a recurring
anxiety that children will be in danger of developing a narrowness
of knowledge and understanding if they learn only that which
arises out of their own concerns, and become involved in the

time-consuming process of self-referencing. There are two things that need to be said immediately to this, before raising a more serious dilemma that this point presents to us.

The first is a reminder that we should be wary of supposing that children's real concerns, as against their more superficial wants and surface interests, are likely to be narrow in scope. This point was developed in the previous chapter.

The second is that, of course the teacher has a role to play in provoking and stimulating new thoughts and concerns. Developing a child's authenticity is not to be equated with stultification and teacher passivit. How could it be when so many other aspects of a child's experience and social environment are actively shaping his or her ideas in all sorts of ways – sometimes for the worse? As has been previously emphasized in the notion of 'empathetic challenging', respect for authenticity is *not* advocation of passivity and the laissez-faire, but is more to do with accepting that the child is the final arbiter of what is making sense, and the conditions under which things can acquire personal significance. Children's concerns are the touchstone of their learning, not its completion.

We now come up against what I think is the real issue at stake: the notion of self-referencing places emphasis on the value of *depth* of thought at the expense of *breadth*. But instrumental considerations apart, why should breadth be preferred to depth? Straight rationalism in both its 'hard' and 'soft' forms would claim that lack of introduction into a wide range of areas of knowledge is an obvious deprivation, and runs counter to a child's 'entitlement'. But, on the other hand, it seems plausible to argue that real understanding and its associated insights, satisfactions, and challenges to think, only come with depth and sustained involvement with a relatively limited range of issues. Heidegger once made a remark to the effect that every great thinker thinks one thought, rethinking it and re-expressing it again and again from a variety of perspectives and through its many ramifications. Surely there is some truth in this which has application to lesser mortals? Would it not be thinking of this sustained and focused kind which would generate the attitudes necessary for full engagement with an issue, including the authentic evaluation of what one learns, and which therefore constitutes personal growth and carries one fruitfully into new situations? Such attitudes are in stark contrast with those which go along with compendium knowledge acquisition. In his famous attack on the transmission of 'inert ideas' in education, A. N. Whitehead beseeched us to guard against such 'mental dry rot':

> We enunciate two educational commandments, 'Do not teach too many subjects,' and again, 'What you teach, teach thoroughly.' . . . The result of teaching small parts of a large number of subjects is the passive reception of disconnected ideas, not illumined with any spark of vitality. Let the main ideas which are introduced into a child's education be few and important, and let them be thrown into every combination possible. The child should make them his own, and should understand their application here and now in the circumstances of his actual life.[6]

In the light of such considerations, and in a situation where in reality a choice is to be made between children having breadth of knowledge as, say, advocated by Hirst, Bailey, or the nine foundation subjects and myriad attainment objectives of the National Curriculum, and quality of understanding in terms of depth of personal significance required by authentic learning, why should we assume that the latter constitutes a greater deprivation than the former? Is someone who, say, knows only enough maths, science, history and geography to get by in a practical everyday way, but has a deep personal understanding and love of literature and music, really deprived or less adequate as a person compared with someone who, relatively speaking, has a superficial formal understanding of all these things? For the moment I will simply leave this as an issue for the reader to consider.

But such a line of thought does suggest a certain general methodology for producing the content of a child's education. It is what one might term the method of 'depth sampling'. By this I mean that instead of trying to cover the seemingly endless ground of what 'in the abstract' may be thought to be important for children to know, we treat what is taught as *exemplars*: as themes that have the potential to illustrate both what a broader area of study has to offer in terms of its human significance, and something of its depth structure (central concepts, ideas and procedures) so as to encourage early active engagement. In keeping with the notion of self-referencing, the detailed selection, i.e. what becomes treated in this way, will depend crucially on its potential to develop and refine that which motivates children's deeper interests and concerns. But in this way it may be that a fair degree of what is representative of a broader curriculum may be achieved at a level which is intellectually challenging and personally satisfying. For, given that culture has itself grown out of attempts to articulate and understand human concerns, and, as we have noted, in turn conditions the kinds of concerns it is possible to have, it would be odd indeed if there was not a large degree of coincidence between the more developed forms of thinking within culture and the felt needs of children in pursuing their concerns.

Now I suspect that this approach is not such a far cry from what many of those who originally sat on the separate subject committees to produce proposals for the content of the National Curriculum had in mind – at least in some degree. But the cumulative effect of their proposals, and the interpretation and modifications sometimes subsequently placed on them, endanger the survival of this element. It is, then, of the greatest importance that the approach should be defended. Not, of course, that this could be expected to change (in the short term at least) the legislated curriculum framework with which the primary school has now to comply. But it might affect the spirit in which the curriculum requirements are interpreted in practice and this could be of the greatest importance. What scope there may be for this is taken up in Chapter 12.

NOTES AND REFERENCES

1 Some of the broader issues relating to moral values in school are explored in Bottery (1990).
2 Some of the underlying ideas in this section have been developed in more depth in Bonnett (1978).
3 See, for example, Elliott (1975) for an important discussion of this issue and his development of the notion of the 'intimidating power of orthodoxy' of the disciplines. These themes are also taken up by Cooper (1983), pp. 58–63, who relates them to a critique of the whole idea of the disciplines being 'rule-governed'.
4 Matthews (1980), p. 28.
5 Kierkegaard (1843).
6 Whitehead (1932), pp. 2–3.

CHAPTER 11
Poetic Thinking

The world is too much with us: late and soon,
Getting and spending, we lay waste our powers;
Little we see in Nature that is ours;
We have given our hearts away . . .
William Wordsworth

In the previous chapter I looked at some ways in which the objection of self-centredness might be pressed against authentic-rational thinking. Is the notion of self-referencing – now conceived as a determination not to subject everything to personal whim, but to refer things to one's self so that one genuinely responds to what one encounters and thus makes one's understanding of it one's own – sufficient to characterize the kind of thinking and understanding with which education should be primarily concerned?

As it stands, it is not clear that it is. Just as straight rationalism seems to pay too little attention to the element of individuality in thinking and the importance of subjective weight in a proper understanding of non-trivial things, so the notions of self-expression and self-referencing which are at the centre of personal authenticity and authentic–rational thought might seem to underplay a further essential element, namely that of *receptivity*. What I have in mind here is a consideration that we have in fact already briefly touched upon in the discussion of the role of the teacher in Chapter 9, and which is much amplified by 'philosophers of Being'. It is an aspect of the self-centredness issue which is perhaps best brought out by again making reference to some of the features of rationalism noted in Part Two.

The 'calculative' and the 'poetic'

It will be remembered that one of the main ideas to emerge from the analysis given in Part Two was that rationality is not a neutral form of thinking: it involves, often implicitly, a certain project with regard to the world. It seeks to explain, predict, evaluate, and control the environment, i.e. *it is essentially manipulative in motive* – and to this end it represents things to itself through the use of categories which define things in standard ways. That is to say, it turns things themselves into *objects of thought*, which have the properties of the categories to which they have been assigned. Now it has been claimed that this way of thinking is fundamentally unreceptive in that it closes off much of the many-sidedness of the things with which it deals. What can appear for such thinking is only those aspects of the thing pre-specified by the categories applied. Thus we may be predisposed to see, say, a flower not simply as it is in the fullness of its standing there, but as an exemplar of a certain genus, exhibiting certain pre-specified characteristics, the product of a certain evolutionary process, the source of some drug or other commodity, etc. Similarly, it may seem, by requiring that thinking reference things to the concerns and previous experience and understanding of the individual, may not authentic learning also be blinkered to the fullness of what is actually present? May not things be seen in terms of a relatively narrow set of individual aspirations and interests which are possibly even more instrumental in stance than those of the public forms of rationality?

What seems to underlie the objections implied by these questions is some idea that it is possible to relate to things in a more open and unprejudiced manner which will thus allow them to show themselves more fully. That is to say, there seems to be a claim that we can have a more direct awareness of things where what we perceive and think is not exclusively mediated by – and therefore limited by – the public categories we employ and the idiosyncratic or social purposes we may as individuals pursue. Rather there is a form of thinking which springs from *things as they are in themselves*. Such thinking has been termed by Heidegger 'poetic' (also 'meditative') and the claim would be that it involves a mode of relating to things where both rational categories and personal self are in some sense, and to some degree, transcended. All forms of thinking have to make distinctions. What is in question is the extent to which they are essentially a matter of social convention and imposed on reality as against an expression of things themselves and thus truly responsive to reality.[1]

Lest all this is beginning to sound rather esoteric, let me attempt to give some examples of what might count as poetic thinking. Perhaps one of the most powerful ones is when we are struck with wonderment and awe at some aspect of Nature. In such experience we seem to leave behind both our self-orientated interests and our normal everyday categories in terms of which we manage things, and become absorbed by the phenomenon itself. We experience something whose presence by far outstrips our ability to fully grasp or articulate it, and in some sense we simply give ourselves over to celebrating the experience itself. We are there *in* the experience rather than somewhat abstracted from it, as in the case of rational scrutiny, and we are there in a way determined more by the quality of the thing we are relating to than by our personal concerns, as in what I have so far characterized as authentic thinking. An acute awareness of this active 'presencing' of things fills the poetry of Gerard Manley Hopkins:

> As kingfishers catch fire, dragonflies draw flame;
> As tumbled over rim in roundy wells
> Stones ring; like each tucked string tells, each hung bell's
> Bow swung finds tongue to fling out broad its name;
> Each mortal thing does one thing and the same:
> Deals out that being indoors each one dwells;
> Selves – goes itself; *myself* it speaks and spells,
> Crying *What I do is me: for that I came.*[2]

And then again in the following thought which expresses something of the sense of respect and responsibility that is part of such awareness:

> To mend her we end her,
> When we hew or delve:
> After-comers cannot guess the beauty been.
> Ten or twelve, only ten or twelve
> Strokes of havoc unselve
> The sweet especial scene,
> Rural scene, a rural scene,
> Sweet especial rural scene.[3]

A similar phenomenon of becoming involved in the particular can occur in the contemplation of a work of art. Somehow we can get drawn into the work in such a way that our habitual categories and concerns fall away and we experience what may be a familiar thing or situation afresh – see it in a way freed from our everyday associations which average it off and turn it into an ordinary and unremarkable object. The paintings of Vincent van Gogh are perhaps particularly powerful examples of attempts to portray the vital presence or 'thingness' of things. Take his painting of a chair. We are not invited to see it as simply an instance of something you sit on, or a chair of a certain sort as in a catalogue, but as *this* chair with its own unique vibrant qualities – an ambience into which we can be drawn. Entering into a novel, poem, or piece of music has a similar transporting quality which frees us up to receive what is there in its own right.

And again, poetic experiences are sometimes had in the context of human relationships. For example, situations in which we find ourselves genuinely empathizing with another, seeing life from another's point of view, or a love that is whole-hearted, have as a central feature not what we *impose* on another in some pre-specified way, but what we *receive* in our willingness to make ourselves vulnerable and respond caringly to what is there. But perhaps this is all now beginning to sound rather precious. Let me refer to some examples of the kind that Heidegger uses which have a more 'earthy' feel to them.

Heidegger tries to refer us back to a time when our way of relating to things was less aggressive than it is in modern technological society – a time when we took on the role of something more akin to creative midwife to things as against wilful challenger and consumer. For example, he invites us to consider a contrast between the way things were produced by the craftsman of older technologies and the process of modern manufacturing. He takes the example of the making of a sacrificial silver chalice, and suggests that there was a time when the silversmith would not have been conceived of as *the* cause of the production of the chalice, any more than the midwife is *the* cause of the birth of a child. Rather they both have a role of 'co-responsibility' with other powers that are involved, and bring forth something which was in some sense already there, inchoately. In the case of the silversmith this is expressed through his working with the material so as to bring out its own quality – its texture, lustre, colour – and with the creative forces of the tradition and the culture within which his work has meaning. He does not decide and fix beforehand the precise properties of the metal required, what the chalice is to look like, what is or is not sacrificial, but participates in the interplay of these enabling forces – responsively gathering them on a particular occasion so as to bring *this* chalice into appearance. His creativity and his making are a result of his receptivity, his evolving feel for the powers he is working with and with which he assumes joint responsibility for what is made. And his essential attitude towards things is one of 'working with', co-operation with Nature and culture, rather than 'working upon' which is an expression of self-will.

This, Heidegger feels, can be contrasted with modern manufacturing which fabricates objects according to some pre-given blueprint set up by man's self-will. Here the object is the product of a challenging rather than a responding, and the chief problem is how to produce the maximum yield for the minimum outlay. We can perhaps see this stance as being in part reflected by the kinds of materials modern making favours, such as plastics, which are almost infinitely malleable and require a minimum of 'working with' in the sense outlined above. We try to design materials to satisfy our purposes rather than allow our purposes to be modulated by, and find creative expression through, the qualities of the materials. Our attitude is not one of an on-going responding during the process of making, but of demanding and imposing: What is wanted in all its significant detail is decided in advance of the process of making, and Nature is then challenged to provide the necessary resources for the processing which is to be set in train.

A parallel can be found in modern agriculture. Here again, the stance is basically demanding and manipulative. Our attitude is one of engineering materials (e.g. plants) and conditions to meet our self-given purposes in as efficient a manner as possible. Factory farming techniques in meat and egg production perhaps provide particularly gross expressions of this general underlying attitude. Heidegger suggests a contrast between this and the way in which we engaged in farming in earlier times:

The field that the peasant formerly cultivated and set in order appears different from how it did when to set in order still meant to take care of and maintain. The work of the peasant does not challenge the soil of the field. In sowing grain it places seed in the keeping of the forces of growth and watches over its increase.[4]

The central point that Heidegger is trying to draw to our attention here is not that there was some past 'Golden Age', to which we should try to return, but simply that with older technology the relation to things was one of attendance, an acceptance that Nature would dispose in her own way and in her own good time, such that her integrity would be preserved and revealed. In such a way of relating our being is very much bound to Nature rather than being set apart and imposed upon it. And in this way our thinking is more respectful and revealing of what is there, for what is subjugated does not reveal itself, and we do not live in harmony with something by seeking to manipulate, 'manage' and master it.

These, then, are but examples of two distinct ways of relating to the world. One is termed by Heidegger 'calculative' because it tries to 'reckon everything up' in terms of categories and theories which serve its various self-given projects. This would include many aspects of rational and authentic–rational thinking as characterized in previous discussion. The other, as we have noted, he termed 'poetic' because of its receptive and open stance to things themselves.

There are many other examples that could be drawn upon to illustrate how these two attitudes towards the world can express themselves in everyday living. I will take one more: the way we think of each other. In some contexts we are increasingly encouraged to think of people as a resource, as 'manpower', with all that this brings in its train for how they should be treated: an invitation to exchange and switch them about with no regard for the individuality of those so labelled. Unfortunately, it is not difficult to recognize important parallels here for the ways in which the teacher–pupil relationship can be conceived of in the context of a uniform and externally imposed curriculum. Such possibilities will be explored in later chapters. But what must be said at this point is that, of course, in concrete human existence these dimensions of thinking are matters of degree, and it is not to be supposed that they exist in their pure forms. Much is hybrid. Rather, the claim is that we can formally distinguish between such modes, that they represent significantly different ways of relating to and revealing the world, and that in modern technological society the calculative mode is very much in the ascendent, to the extent even that it makes the poetic appear unfamiliar and archaic, or worse, a frothy irrelevance to the real business of life.[5]

It is perhaps possible to summarize the differences between calculative and poetic thinking in the following way. Firstly their stance towards things:

Calculative	Poetic
self-purposeful	celebratory
goal-orientated	openly curious, wondering
analyses things into problems to be solved	intuits the wholeness of things and receives them as they are
turns things into defined objects – manageable, familiar	stays with things in their inherent strangeness

Secondly, the two kinds of thinking can be characterized by the feelings and aspirations that they elicit:

Calculative	Poetic
satisfaction as a result of sense of sorting things out, getting things ordered, made clear, transparent	sense of mystery, awe, wonder, fascination; evokes feelings of attunement
effects things	affected by things
seeks control	allows itself to be vulnerable
makes statements	'sings', 'says' what is
seeks truth as correctness	seeks truth as revealing

Poetic truth

The final reference to different kinds of truth in the above list is very important, and in many ways lies at the base of the differences between the two modes of thinking, and what would be involved in developing them. Rational thinking seeks to express itself in statements which are correct – meaning by this that they have been tested for their validity against public tests for truth. In principle a statement is either true or false in these terms; it is assumed that at the end of the day there is a correct answer (even if we don't know what it is at present). In contrast to this, the poetic view of truth is simply that of things coming to disclose themselves as they are, rather than how we choose to represent them to ourselves through statements of what is the case in the ways, for example, emphasized by Paul Hirst. There are no correct or incorrect answers because there are no answers at all: in this mode we are not in the business of calculating – we do not set ourselves specific problems to be resolved. We are not, to refer to Bacon's characterization of modern experimental science at its inception, 'putting Nature on the rack' of interrogation, but simply trying to be open to what is there and allow that reality to affect us and provide us with a sense of what is fitting and what not.

Expressions of poetic thinking, therefore, do not give us information – data to be inserted in some argument, theory or formula – but in essence simply 'sing' or 'say' things so as to point us to things themselves and invite participation in them. If they were simply informative statements in the rational sense, the idea of, say, returning to a poem, piece of literature or artwork, or listening to a song, again and again would be as senseless as returning to a reference manual whose information we had already assimilated. In the poetic mode an expression such as 'trees dancing against the sky' states no proposition to be learnt up, gives no information which is correct or incorrect; it simply says or sings an aspect of experience which we can enter into, celebrate, be affected by. The pre-Socratic philosopher Parmenides described this thinking as a native 'letting-lie-before-us and a taking-to-heart'. It is only when we fall out of harmony with things that we set them up as problematic and in need of manipulation. Thus *developing* this kind of thinking will be a very different enterprise to that of developing rational thinking. But before we move on to this issue, we must confront a prior question: why bother? If poetic thinking does not provide us with answers to our problems what use can it be, why should it be considered at all important enough to spend valuable time on in school?

The 'use' of poetic thinking

There are a number of things that may be said in this regard. Perhaps the first is that to raise the question in the above form is already to have taken up the stance of calculative rationality: we are seeking an instrumental value for such thinking in order to justify it. From the perspective of poetic thinking this is to have begged the fundamental question about the purpose of thinking, and its reply would be that it may be less a case of how we can use such thinking, and more a case of *how it might use us*. That is to say, the question is raised as to why we should assume that the only way of making progress, of ameliorating the conditions in which we live and giving our lives meaning, is to assume the mastery. There are traditions which hold that the inspiration which comes from service to something recognized as infinitely greater than ourselves, and through which we achieve a freedom, dignity, and worth larger than any we can manufacture for ourselves, is a fuller realization of human nature. Further, have we not at least been given pause to question the manifest success of the calculative aspect of rational thinking in terms of its devastating consequences for the environment? Does Heidegger put it too strongly when he claims that before we annihilate things in actions we have already annihilated them in thought, i.e. turned them into objects at our disposal, and the latter is a condition of the former occurring?

The central point in all this is that surely we need to consider carefully the implications of our basic stance in thought for our relationship with all around us. Does it embody a fundamental lack of respect for things themselves? If, however implicitly, we assume the earth is there for our use, that we can possess it and have the right to interrogate and exploit it so as to fulfil our own self-given purposes, clearly this sets as a norm a very self-centred view of human being which will colour our perception of all that we do – lead us to identify problems in a certain way and seek solutions of a certain kind. For example, increasingly, conservation and environmental issues would be described and weighed in terms of what is thought to be to the long-term advantage of human beings, rather than of things themselves. The motive for protecting endangered species would be largely in terms of them having some, perhaps as yet unknown, potential to serve us in some manner, and attempts will be made to manage the problem accordingly – maybe by creating convenient sanctuaries or reserves. Rather different solutions might suggest themselves if a genuine respect for things themselves was operative – approaches that involved modification of human aspirations so as to enable us to live harmoniously alongside things. This could be very important. We have little opportunity to develop a proper feel for things, that are hived off in reserves; indeed, in this way they are turned into curios and even more forcefully set up as being at our disposal and requiring our management.

And there is another danger. Such fundamental self-centred-ness leads to a form of nihilism which is already manifesting itself in our everyday lives. The rampant growth of consumerism, it might be claimed, is only the becoming explicit of underlying motives which have always been present implicitly in rational–calculative thinking. Material growth and consumption becoming ends in themselves is simply an expression of the self-will which is embedded in such thinking, and the ultimate sterility that it leads to is simply a feature of a thinking which is increasingly closed in upon itself and can no longer be inspired by meaning and values outside those it has provided for itself. For inspiration precisely consists in being held in the sway of something beyond oneself, outside the current compass of one's thinking – something distinctly *other* – which thus brings a new dimension, vital and strange, into our life. A thinking which predisposes us, no matter how covertly, to seek control by constantly pre-shaping our interactions is in grave danger of retracing increasingly hollow circles. Any originality that it possesses will be of a peculiarly constipated kind.[6]

Thus it may well be, then, that a recognition of poetic thinking is needed not just for our material welfare (and possibly survival), but for our spiritual welfare. To meet the problems that now confront us we may need a radical change of heart, a radical de-centring which rationality in its modern calculative form systematically denies, but covers over by its claims to be objective and impartial. Finally, on a somewhat less elevated plane, the sense of wholeness that poetic thinking can give may be essential to our sense of personal well-being. This is nicely described by William Barrett in the following way:

> I take walks in the woods near where I live; and if I take a walk in those woods in an afternoon I am thinking all the time. But if I come back, and someone says: 'What problem did you solve?' I would say: 'I wasn't doing that kind of thinking. I was ruminating, orientating myself to myself and to Nature.' I feel much more sound and whole when I come back from that sort of reflection. But you can imagine the other person thinking to himself: 'That's very strange. He says he was thinking, yet he wasn't considering any problem and he didn't calculate anything.'[7]

The value of poetic thinking lies not in specific and tangible results or conclusions that follow logically from it, but rather from a sense of attunement, place, and fittingness that it engenders, and within the ambience of which, the rational–calculative systems and arguments in terms of which we have become habituated into thinking of ourselves, need to be re-located in order for their broader significance to be understood and for them to become re-humanized in a deeper sense. This re-orientation is often very subtle and not something of which we may be very consciously aware. Yet it can on occasion be very powerful and explicit as when, for example, the image of a starving child may cause us to adjust our sense of financial or political priorities, or that of a single oil-covered bird our sense of what risks we should be prepared to take with the environment.

Poetic thinking, then, can help to reveal the ground in which our rational calculations are rooted and give us a sense of our own rootedness, or its lack. Through developing our capacity to enter into the very being of things themselves, to be affected by them, we apprehend the underlying qualities of the human world which should ultimately condition our purposes and give weight to our reasonings.

Developing poetic thinking

If the central features of poetic thinking are openness and responsiveness, it does not make sense to conceive of its development
in any pre-structured way that parallels the way we might still
be tempted to think of the development of rational thinking. It
is doubtful that we should conceive of the development of poetic
thinking as a series of definable steps at all because it does not
have at its kernel a set of logical relations articulated in conceptual
schemes. Rather we are concerned with the degree of development of certain qualities and attitudes which the child exhibits in
his or her natural dealings with the world. I attempted to list these
qualities of thought earlier in this chapter, but how are they
acquired?

Well, to begin with, clearly not simply through instruction:
being told about such attitudes and having them explained in
some formal way is a far cry from actually acquiring them, as we
know only too well in an analogous way in the area of moral
education. And unlike moral education where social pressure is
constantly present and sanctions can be applied to 'correct' wrong
behaviour, there are no such unpleasant consequences to be
immediately felt for ignoring the poetic. Quite the reverse. In
terms of the currently dominant instrumental values of efficiency
and mastery, those attitudes which I have associated with the
poetic appear as something of a dispensable sideshow. Exhorta-
tion, then, has small chance of success, and indeed would in any
case be contrary to the nature of poetic thinking itself. Rather,
it would seem, the child needs to rub shoulders with people who
themselves value such thinking, who allow it to influence their
lives: give it space and time, somewhat in the manner discussed
earlier in relation to initiating children into the living traditions
of thought described by Michael Oakeshott (pp. 45-6).

Thus, teacher and children might share a sense of wonder and
astonishment at, say, the sheer variety, complexity and beauty
of micro-organisms in a drop of pond water; the sheer magnitude
of distances and masses in human terms in the solar system or
the galaxy, the sheer vibrancy or intensity or softness of a colour;
the sheer ambience of a particular place or situation; the sheer
courage, tenacity, selfishness, etc. of an historical or fictional

character; the sheer evocativeness or transporting power of a piece of music; and so on. Throughout, the power of metaphor to mix, and break the hold of, rational categories so as to invite fresh responses might be highlighted. A teacher who valued the poetic would give ample time to simply experience, celebrate, and express such ways of relating to things before they get incorporated into some cosy classification or computer data-base which neutralizes their particularity and tranquillizes their strangeness, by turning them into instances of generalities. In such classification, analysis and explanation, it is easy, too, for the quiet beauty and wonder of things familiar and near at hand to be covered over, for in rational ordering it is the overarching *idea* or concept that sets the pace and the thing itself is in danger of silently vanishing from view. A gross example of this might be when, say, the living quality of a particular colour becomes transmuted through analysis and explanation into a mere mathematical wavelength.

In many ways, then, the poetic outlook must be caught rather than taught in any didactic sense. Though not simply this, for many of the qualities and attitudes which constitute the poetic, such as wholehearted involvement and sense of wonderment, seem to be exhibited quite naturally by many young children, and therefore it is often a matter of maintaining and enlarging something that is already present as against introducing something alien. Sensitive provision of opportunity, evocative images, experiences and situations, encouragement, and genuine (i.e. *open*) conversation are the ways in which an appeal can be made to the poetic aspects of a child's nature such that it can consolidate itself and grow. Here, of course, the arts have much to offer, *if treated in the right spirit*, i.e. not as things to be learnt up or evaluated in a rational/critical mode, but as things to be entered into and felt. Free, though not undisciplined, participation in poetry, literature, art, music, drama are vital forms of poetic thought, as is the sense of wonderment in the face of natural phenomena and certain human artifacts previously mentioned. But the term 'free' here now refers less to existentialist notions of self-conscious and deliberated choice and decision as to uninhibited and wholehearted involvement in which a person is inspired by, and carried along by, their engagement. Their thinking is uninhibited not in the sense that any old response will do, but in the sense that it is 'commissioned by Being', is apt to things themselves rather than operating through imposed systems. This capacity to enter into, and experience wonder in, the things around us is perhaps the best protection against the insatiable appetite for cheap sensationalism which is its corrupted counterpart.

Nonetheless, there remains a sense in which authentic choice remains a constituent part of poetic thinking: it is closely associated with the nature of this rigour of poetic thinking and involves the quality of responsibility inherent in authentic choice being shown towards things themselves so that they may be truly revealed. Some of this has already been hinted at earlier in this chapter (for example, in our discussion of Heidegger's 'crafts-man'), but I think the issues here are particularly difficult, and since it is not strictly necessary to enter them in order to engage in the topics covered in the remaining chapters, I will not pursue them here. I have placed some discussion of them in an appendix for any reader with sufficient inclination – and stamina – to wish to take them further![8] At this point, rather than pursuing the arguments in more depth, it would be useful to take stock of the position that has now been reached by drawing together some of the diverse strands that have been explored.

A summary: dimensions of understanding

It is clear that thinking has many facets and that in many ways it is best thought of as a generic term embracing significantly different kinds which exhibit or emphasize differing qualities and characteristics. 'Rational–calculative', 'authentic' and 'poetic' have been suggested as examples of such forms which in turn give rise to differing qualities and levels of understanding. If, then, we wished to analyse a child's existing understanding in order to diagnose its strengths and weaknesses – to identify where lacks and problems are arising so as to attempt to make them good – it could be useful to examine it from the point of view of the differing facets which our examination has brought into view. In Figure 11.1 on p. 142, I have attempted to set out some of the factors that have now been identified as constitutive of

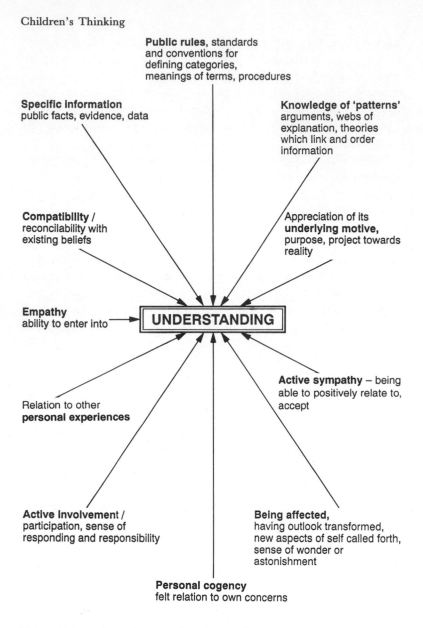

Figure 11.1 Constituents of understanding.

understanding. Clearly there are strong possibilities of overlap with regard to the qualities shown, and equally, which of them is appropriate will depend on the context – for example, that which is to be understood. Those components applicable to, say, a proper understanding of a mathematical calculation are likely to differ from those applicable to the understanding of a poem or human relationship. But by becoming more sensitive to those particular qualities which are constitutive of the understanding we wish to develop, we put ourselves in a better position to properly evaluate the provision we are making in the tasks and experiences we offer children. For example, is Sarah's difficulty in understanding *Macbeth* rooted in a lack of comprehension of some of the language in which it is couched ('meaning of terms'), her difficulty in putting herself in Macbeth's shoes, her inability to muster any active sympathy for his outlook, her difficulty in seeing its underlying motive etc . . ., or some combination of any of these or more? Such interrelated, but significantly distinct aspects, may each require differing kinds of support, discussion etc. if enhanced quality of understanding is to be achieved.

NOTES AND REFERENCES

1 See some of the later works of Heidegger, such as the collections of essays *Poetry, Language, Thought* (1971), and *The Question Concerning Technology and Other Essays* (1977); also *Discourse on Thinking* (1969).

2 From G. Manley Hopkins, *The Major Poems*, ed. Walford Davies (1979), p. 87.

3 Ibid., p. 76: 'Binsey Poplars'.

4 'The Question Concerning Technology', op. cit.

5 I have attempted to develop these ideas in their relation to education in 'Education in a destitute time' (1983).

6 Although coming from very different perspectives, such concerns over the perceived tendencies in discursive rationality to insulate, uproot and mechanize thinking have been expressed by many thinkers. For example, D. H. Lawrence argued that thinking through the medium of 'trains of ideas' prevents us from living more spontaneously, and therefore more truly, out of our 'vital affective centres' (e.g. in 'Education of the people', 1936) and he vigorously attacks what he takes to be the cheap instrumentalism and the stultifying effect of rationality in general in the polemical 'Benjamin Franklin' (1923), both in Williams and Williams (1973). See, also, the very useful discussion of Lawrence on these issues in Bantock (1952), Ch. 6.

A particularly vehement attack on the uprooting aspect of modern rationality at its inception in the thinking of Socrates was mounted by Nietzsche in *Twilight of the Idols*. He accused Socrates of making a tyrant of reason, which reflected the destroyed trust in the vital instinctive life. Criticizing Socrates' elevation of dialectics – the pursuit of truth through rational argument and debate – and his 'phony' equation of 'reason = virtue = happiness', Nietzsche writes:

> With Socrates Greek taste undergoes a change in favour of dialectics: what is really happening when this happens? It is above all the defeat of a *nobler* taste. . . . Before Socrates, the dialectical manner was repudiated in good society: it was regarded as a form of bad manners, one was compromised by it. Young people were warned against it. And all such presentation of one's reasons was regarded with mistrust. Honest things, like honest men, do not carry their reasons exposed in this fashion. It is indecent to display all one's goods. What has first to have itself proved is of little value . . . (p. 41)

7 Barrett (1978).
8 I have also explored them in 'Personal authenticity and public standards', in Cooper (1986). See also an interesting discussion of a number of issues that relate to my position on this point and the general theme of this chapter in Standish (1992), Chs 5 and 6.

Part Four
The Role of the Teacher in Developing Children's Thinking

CHAPTER 12

The Place of Structure in Developing Children's Thinking

In recent years there has been much emphasis on the need to thoroughly structure children's work in the primary school. This movement has largely been a reaction to what was perceived as the excesses of child-centred or progressive education, where lack of continuity and progression were considered to pervade what children were doing. This in turn led to many attempts to provide more detailed guidelines and schemes of work in the various school subjects or 'areas of experience' by such bodies as the former Schools Council and some Local Education Authorities so as to ensure a more systematic approach to children's learning. And now, of course, we have moved into a period where greater national uniformity is being sought through the legislation contained in the Education Reform Act of 1988.

As is well known, this legislation sets out a detailed national curriculum in terms of the areas of study to be covered in all state-maintained schools, and the attainment targets to be achieved within each of these areas by the end of the period of compulsory schooling. Within this broad framework various 'key stages' have been erected in terms of children's ages, with their associated 'levels' and detailed 'statements of attainment' and 'programmes of study'. Related to these is a set of procedures for monitoring and communicating children's progress, centring on the continuous assessment of the teacher and a battery of 'standard assessment tasks', which are administered at end of each key stage. In this way it is intended to 'raise standards' in education and to provide a comprehensive record of what each individual child has achieved during his or her progress through the system.

With regard to the primary age range, which is our main concern here, the outline arrangements amount to the following: each child will study the three 'core subjects' of English, Maths and Science, and in addition the other 'foundation subjects' of Technology (including design), History, Geography, Music, Art, and Physical Education. Further, all schools must make provision for religious education, and certain cross-curricular themes, such as those relating to Health, Environment, and Citizenship. Each of the core and foundation subjects has its own overall targets of attainment specifying a number of general aspects to be studied, and each target is broken down into five or six levels felt appropriate to span the primary age range. Each of these levels is itself then broken down into a number of more specific statements of attainment. It is anticipated that the average child will achieve the attainments set out in Level 4 by the end of his or her junior schooling, with a range of two levels either side to cover the extremes of the less and the more able.

Clearly we have here, then, a very detailed prescribed curriculum which maps the paths of children's learning across a broad range of subjects independently of any individual child. In the light of previous discussion a clear and pressing question arises: how compatible is this degree of pre-specification with the principles that have emerged from our consideration of the development of authentic–rational and poetic thinking? Before answering this question directly, I would like to locate it in a broader framework of considerations.

Five sources of structure for children's learning

There are a large number of considerations that intimately affect the way children's learning is structured in the primary school. Many are of a highly practical nature: for example, the availability of staff and equipment, the timetabling of certain key rooms, such as the hall or AVA room, the particular published schemes that are currently on hand. But underlying such practical issues are a number of more fundamental points of reference for decisions concerning the structuring of children's learning. I believe it is possible to identify five such underlying structuring principles that in varying degree and combination commonly serve this role, and which it would therefore be useful to examine from the perspectives developed in this book.

Firstly, there is what one might call the *individual teacher's viewpoint*. By this I refer to the way a particular teacher's conception of what should be taught might influence the content, style and direction of the children's work. It will reflect the personal associations that the teacher makes between different items of learning, her values, her enthusiasms, her felt strengths. This point of reference may sometimes determine only the degree of emphasis placed on different aspects of what is taught or how it is taught, but may on occasion determine much of the framework for learning, as say in a project largely devised by the teacher. The point is that structure is provided by the teacher's personal perception of what is valuable, needed, possible, enjoyable, etc.

In evaluating this source of structure we might be tempted to say simply that it has the advantage of maximizing teacher commitment but the disadvantage of risking a considerable degree of idiosyncrasy. Yet while there must be some truth in this, it is not quite so straightforward. Let us think back to some of the considerations raised in Parts Two and Three. Oakeshott's view of education, for example, strongly suggests a sense in which the teacher should be regarded as to some significant degree an individual *embodiment* of the culture and traditions into which we may wish to introduce children. Through her individuality she exhibits a particular way in which they have become integrated into a human life and therefore, to the extent that she is authentic, she is capable of displaying to children what an honest engagement with them might mean – how they make a difference to what we see and feel. Now this can become apparent not only in the role model she provides in her day-to-day interaction with her class (important though this is) but also in her on-going selection of content. Through this latter, by deciding certain priorities and giving certain emphases, she can bring an area of study into relief, a relief which expresses the life of an area through being imbued with *her* life – her sense of what is important, problematic, analogous, interesting, fascinating or a source of wonderment. It seems to me that this potentially important source of integration and vitality in what we present to children should not be lightly overridden.

The second principle, or point of reference, for structuring children's work is the *structure of knowledge* itself. The idea here is that if we examine the realm of public knowledge available to us today we will see that it has its own logical structure of facts, concepts and procedures, which children need to acquire if they are to gain systematic and disciplined knowledge and understanding. The rationalist view of knowledge discussed in Part Two (especially that of Hirst) would be a paradigm example of such an approach, and it is reflected in many published schemes of work, particularly in the areas of maths and science, where children may follow a prescribed path for learning step by step, page by page, card by card. etc. (It is important to recall here, however, that such linearity of learning was radically called into question by the more sophisticated forms of rationalism we considered in Part Two.) This principle ensures that a certain content is covered in a systematic way and has the further advantage of focusing on what we may call the 'depth structure' of knowledge – the underlying concepts and procedures that one needs to acquire in order to participate in an area of knowledge rather than be a passive receiver of information only. But as such it makes no direct reference to what is seen as interesting or relevant by the learner. While it certainly allows for matching between child and task, this is seen in terms of ability only, and then only in narrowly conceived terms which takes little heed of the extent to which the child's own motivation and quality of engagement can actually *determine* perceived ability. Further, as was pointed out in Chapter 4, there is the danger of such knowledge losing its organic feel if it is subject to a detailed analytic dissection into components, and that poetic understanding – because it is not susceptible to this kind of analysis – will be heavily distorted or ignored altogether.

The third approach is what one might call the *skills-centred principle*, an approach which has become closely associated with so-called 'process' views of the curriculum. Here the idea is that there are a number of important skills that children need to learn – relatively independently of any particular knowledge content – which will enable them to operate effectively in a wide range of situations and to find out, evaluate, and generate knowledge for themselves. For this reason their acquisition has sometimes been denoted by the epithet 'learning how to learn'. The 'communication skills' of reading and writing would be a case in point, but also a wide range of so-called 'thinking skills' such as hypothesizing, interpreting, evaluating, etc.; 'observation skills' in art and science; 'social skills' required to get on with people, down to very specific skills such as being able to use an index or a pair of scissors. This emphasis on know-how as against know-that often brings an overtly instrumental, and sometimes vocational element to the structuring of children's learning. Learning is not done for its own sake, i.e. out of some sense of its intrinsic worth, but as a means to some further purpose. Alone, this principle runs the danger of leading to skills being learnt in a relatively mechanical way through lacking a sufficient context of understanding to guide application – and, indeed, to give them intellectual structure in the case of 'thinking skills'. Further, as with the knowledge-centred principle, there is the danger of them remaining unrelated to the concerns of an individual child so that their value is not felt and the possession of them is not *in fact* empowering.

Now a feature shared by each of the sources of structure so far described is that they are essentially *closed*: they attempt to prescribe in advance what is to be learnt. For this reason they lend themselves well to a way of structuring learning that sets out clearly-defined objectives which give both a strong sense of direction, and reference points against which work can be monitored and progress measured. This, in turn, can give a sense of security in knowing that 'the ground is being covered' and facilitates clear organization of teaching and resources. Learning structured in this way gives the impression of having been well thought through and efficiently administered, and clearly this impression has appealed strongly to the authors of the Education Reform Act. The remaining two principles are potentially far more open-ended in character.

The first of these is where the *investigation of some real problem or issue* becomes the point of reference for what is learnt. Such investigations may be into some aspect of the local environment (e.g. issues concerning where to place a new by-pass, the design of some local amenity, etc.), or drawn from life in some broader respect (e.g. the plight of the Third World, endangered species, pollution), or then again, much narrower in focus, such as a specific maths investigation. The point is that when this principle assumes dominance, the structure of children's work is provided by the enquiry itself – content and direction develop according to wherever the enquiry happens to lead.

The advantage of this approach is held to be that it endows the work with a realism and relevance to normal life and better reflects the character of human endeavour. On the other hand, depending on the particular issues chosen for investigation, it may not cover the ground in a sufficiently thorough and systematic way when viewed from the perspective some of the other principles of structure previously mentioned. Also, it is important to notice that while the problem-centred approach is clearly open-ended in a significant sense, it is not necessarily so from *the standpoint of the pupil*. Certainly, precise learning outcomes are not pre-specified – rather they emerge as the enquiry develops – but it remains the case that the problem itself could be, and often is, initiated by the teacher, and its development determined by his or her view of what needs to be done. This being so, teacher-, knowledge-, skills- and problem-centred approaches, while providing structure in a fairly clear sense and thus providing a fairly firm basis for planning for coherence and continuity, of course do this only from within their own perspective. Such perspectives, which represent points of reference external to the learner, take little account of the possibility that one person's coherence can be another person's confusion, i.e. that different individuals have different concerns and learning styles, and make sense of things in different ways.[1]

This consideration brings me to the last of the principles I am going to consider as a source of structure in the work of the child: namely that of the *consciousness of the child him- or herself*. By this I refer to that subjective structure of beliefs, understandings, and concerns which constitute the child's own outlook on the world, and in terms of which he or she has ultimately to make sense of what is learnt if it is to gain the kind of subjective weight discussed in previous chapters. Clearly this principle will always be operative to some degree, whatever other sources of structure we seek to impose on the child's work. The question it poses is the extent to which we seek to celebrate it, or ignore or repress it – and the extent that it will therefore find positive or negative expression in the child's response to the work.

From the point of view of developing thinking and understanding it is perhaps open to two central objections. The first is that interpreted in the way that it has been by some proponents of the 'child-centred' or 'progressive' tradition in education it could lead to work of a very superficial nature. Our previous discussions on the nature and value of self-expression and authenticity have made it clear that not any old whim or transient interest should constitute the touchstone of learning. Nor even, straightforwardly, the child's everyday way of being. We may recall that it was argued that as far as possible we should be actively seeking to identify, explore and refine those *deeper* concerns which a child may have, and which in time give an increasing sense of personal engagement and responsibility in learning.

Now in the light of these important qualifications might it not be reasonable to suggest that it would be better to simply abandon the term 'child-centred' in order to avoid inviting unwanted associations with the laissez-faire in education? I'm not myself convinced that this would be best. To begin with, the great thinkers in the child-centred tradition such as Rousseau and Dewey have never advocated a totally laissez-faire approach. Practices of this kind, to the extent that they have ever achieved a reality beyond the caricatured portrayals of those hostile to the tradition, have largely arisen on the basis of misunderstandings of its underlying philosophy. To abandon the term on this basis, then, would be to provide yet another example of not allowing issues of truth to pervert the course of dogma. But also, no really satisfactory alternative labels come to mind. I'm not sure that terms such as, say, 'learner-centred' or 'pupil-centred' either sufficiently escape these associations, nor, which is very important, do they do justice to the way our discussion of authentic learning emphasized its essential relationship to life in a broader sense than that picked out by thinking of someone as a 'learner' or 'pupil'. I intend, then, to stick with the term 'child-centred' on the understanding that it is to be interpreted in the qualified way I have tried to develop.

The second objection is that the child-centred principle, even thus interpreted, could clearly lead to an idiosyncratic and narrow path of learning when viewed from the standpoint of the public forms of knowledge. But the arguments concerning its strengths and weaknesses in this regard have already been explored in our discussion of the issue of breadth versus depth in children's learning (pp. 124–7) and so I will not rehearse them again here. How the child-centred principle might actually be brought to bear explicitly in the planning of children's work is a matter to which I will return presently.

For the moment, it is important to be clear on another point: in no way is it being suggested that in practice the five principles I have sketched are mutually exclusive. The structure of a lesson, a scheme of work, a teaching or learning episode, may be influenced by varying combinations of these principles: it is often more a matter of relative emphasis than exclusivity. But to grant this does not in the least undermine the claim that such distinctions can be made and that it is important to make them. An awareness of them can alert us to important questions concerning priorities to be given between them in differing circumstances and ways in which they interrelate in their contribution to developing children's thinking. Indeed, in many regards they relate quite closely to some of the constituents of understanding summarized at the end of the last chapter. The chief function of these principles, then, is to serve as interrelated points of reference in the preparation for, and analysis of, how we develop thinking and understanding. That they *are* interrelated is easily demonstrated in the way that, say, the defining and investigating of problems draws on knowledge and skills, and insofar as the teacher exercises any control over the conditions in which learning takes place, and responds to on-going developments, his or her own perception of what is needed must be operative, etc.

However, this is not to deny that also there can be significant tensions between them which can only be resolved by coming to some decision as to which are the more central to the quality of learning we should be trying to achieve in a particular context. For example, with regard to a particular piece of learning, do the qualities of understanding offered by the problem-centred principle justify the extra outlay of time? Just how great a context of previous knowledge and personal understanding is needed for such and such skill to be effectively taught? Views on such issues, at the very general level of what counts as truly educational learning, have been rehearsed in Parts Two and Three of this work. I will now explore some more detailed considerations by turning to an examination of the National Curriculum.

Structure and the National Curriculum

While there is a certain amount of variation from one foundation subject to another, it is I think true to say that in general the attainment targets and statements of attainment draw heavily on the knowledge- and skills-centred principles of structure, whereas the programmes of study show more recognition of problem-solving and possibly child-centred principles. In one sense one might think that it could hardly be any other way. How can one have specific statements of attainment for genuinely open-ended forms of structure? Is it not quite correct to see a range of prescribed outcomes in terms of knowledge and skills setting the objectives of education while considerations concerning problem- and child-centred principles bear more appropriately on issues of methodology? I wish to suggest that such a view assumes too neat a distinction between ends and means, between the desired outcomes of education and the procedures of education. A consideration of this issue will lead us to address three related questions:

1. What is the relationship between means and ends in the development of children's thinking and understanding?
2. Is it possible to give coherent structure and sense of direction to this development without the detailed pre-specification of objectives of the kind set out in the National Curriculum?
3. Given that all teachers in state-maintained schools have to work within the legal requirements of the National Curriculum legislation, to what extent is there scope for them to structure children's work in the open-ended way which the problem- and child-centred principles advocate?

The main point that I would like to make with regard to the issue of means and ends is that unlike, say, the production of sausages, in which the nature of the processing is not carried forward as an integral part of the end-product, as far as the development of consciousness is concerned, it certainly is. Indeed, the 'outcomes' of mental development are really largely summaries of the paths taken to achieve them. That is to say that in the context of developing thinking and understanding, the means are often *constitutive* of the ends. This can be true in two ways: logically and experientially.

It is true *logically* in the sense that acquiring and developing certain aptitudes and attitudes is only achieved by exercising them. Imagination, or criticalness of mind can be taught in no other way than by exhibiting and practising these powers: there is nothing separate that one can do in developing them which is not an integral part of what it is to have them. Thus the quality of thinking and understanding in such cases is very much an *expression* of the experiences through which they were acquired.

The means can be *experientially* constitutive of the ends in that the exercise of thinking often requires that we bring into play those experiences through which previous understanding was formed. It is a drawing upon these experiences, not some discrete product that exists quite independently of them as in the case of a mechanical skill such as the use of scissors which may make no reference to the contexts in which it was originally learnt. (And even here, *skilful* cutting may on occasion involve bringing to mind past experiences of cutting.) Similarly the affective aspects of thinking and understanding, whose central importance I have previously attempted to bring out in Part Three, feed off the experiences from which they sprang. As well as one's particular attitudes, one's general stance towards things, is very much a carrying forward of the past into the present and the future. One feels the way one does partly through past experiences colouring one's outlook.

Now the important upshot of such considerations is to suggest that the notion that we should go about structuring children's learning by firstly identifying in detail what the end-products are to be and then devise the means invites too mechanical and closed a view as to how thinking develops, and an underestimation of the intrinsic worth of the procedures (means) themselves. That is to say, it assumes that defining ends is both possible and desirable with regard to how people should think, and discounts unquestioningly the possible value of allowing the means, i.e. the procedures and intrinsic direction of on-going experiences, to determine the ends.

Structure without stricture?

The issue of structuring work in the absence of detailed pre-specified learning objectives is one which now has a considerable history. It was perhaps first brought into clear focus by the thinking of Lawrence Stenhouse in relation to the work of the Humanities Curriculum Project.[2] The problem that he addressed there was that of how schools should teach controversial issues, given that pupils were going to come up against them and have to make judgements about them in the world outside school. Stenhouse's point was that in the case of genuinely controversial issues such as, say, abortion, voluntary euthanasia, war, it would be improper for a school to attempt to specify the particular views children should hold, yet clearly they needed to be prepared to face such issues as part of their broader education. In this situation Stenhouse argued that the teacher's role should be to organize discussion which was genuinely open-ended but which reflected certain basic democratic values in terms of its procedures. That is to say, the development of students' thinking in these areas would be structured in terms of such principles as hearing both sides of the story, being made familiar with relevant evidence, listening to and examining each other's attempts to articulate their opinions and rationally justify them. It was held that such *procedural principles* would give a certain structure and quality to the student's experience without prejudicing the outcome in terms of the final beliefs that they came to hold as a result of that experience.[3]

At the kernel of this approach, then, is the notion that learning can be structured without reference to objectives conceived in terms of precise outcomes. Of course, the selection of procedural principles could not be made without reference to certain general aims – in this case the understanding of the issue and the development of independent thinking – but such aims are themselves an expression of the ideal of openness of thought and do not pre-specify a particular content in terms of knowledge and beliefs to be acquired. Rather they suggest what is to be built into *the quality of the experience*, i.e. the kinds of opportunities the experience will provide, leaving it open as to how individuals will respond, and exactly what they will take away from it.

157

How, then might this approach be applied to the primary school as a way of structuring children's learning on a broader front, and so as to express the problem- and child-centred principles? Below I have listed some questions that a teacher concerned to bring these principles to bear in the way she structures learning might ask herself as she comes to plan the experiences she intends to provide for her class:

1. In what ways will she allow/encourage individual pupils to *initiate* their learning activities (e.g. through expression of an interest or concern)? And how will she attempt to assess the degree of authenticity of such concerns?

2. When, and to what extent, will she allow/encourage pupils to *negotiate* their learning activities with her?

3. When and to what extent will she at least *consult* pupils before deciding what she will ask them to do (e.g. by taking them into her confidence and explaining the underlying rationale and relevance to them of what she intends and seeking their opinions)? And to what extent will she consult them after the activity to seek their opinions regarding its success?

4. To what extent will she allow/encourage pupils to *choose* how they will follow up something that she has initiated?

5. To what extent is she prepared to allow pupils to *experiment* and genuinely experience the consequences of their own decisions (e.g. even when they appear to be making 'mistakes')?

6. In what ways will she provide pupils with *challenges* which arise out of, or are relevant to, *their own concerns* and which will require the use of their own initiative?

7. To what extent will she genuinely seek pupils' *own feelings and opinions* and take up and build upon their ideas, e.g. in a discussion situation?

8. To what extent, and under what conditions, might she be prepared to enter 'sensitive areas', for example, to explore with children personal matters to do with, say, concerns they may have about friendship or family relationships, moral and controversial social issues, anxieties about health, illness, death?

9. To what extent will she encourage pupils to discuss and evaluate their own progress in terms that *they* feel are appropriate?

Some of these questions might be further be analysed in terms of pupil choice concerning:

(a) resources and materials they will use;
(b) organization of time;
(c) organization of place;
(d) who they will work with, if anyone;
(e) which skills to employ.

It should be clear from the above list – which is not, of course, exhaustive – that the ways in which the child-centred principle can be brought to bear in practice are many and various, and operate at different levels, thus giving wide scope for the teacher to decide their applicability in differing circumstances. It is likely that the teacher, given that she certainly cannot assume that children (a) are naturally authentic, (b) will want to be authentic, (c) will be encouraged to be authentic by other agencies, would have to be prepared to work at some of these aspects with considerable perseverence in at least some cases. And she may well need to pay just as much attention to the stage an individual child is at with regard to providing situations for making choices, taking responsibility and engaging in deeper personal reflection, as she would with regard to providing work at the appropriate level in, say, maths. But each of the questions on the list focuses on the quality of experience provided for pupils rather than pre-specified learning outcomes, and taken in conjunction with the teacher's assessment of what her children can cope with in terms of freedom, reflection and responsibility, is capable of providing a clear source of structure for their work.

The underlying claim (as I hope has become clear from previous discussion) is not that the other principles of structure should be ignored – indeed, they are essential sources of content for thinking and understanding, contributing as they do a vast realm of knowledge and experience beyond that which the child currently possesses – but that their educational potential can only be realized by bringing what they offer into the ambit of the child's own thought so that he or she can make what they offer more genuinely his or her own. Previous argument suggests that this requires that the child's own deeper concerns play a significant part in structuring learning, and the supposition that we can somehow by-pass this in the interests of 'efficiency' and breadth of coverage – and still avoid superficiality – is to engage in a convenient but dangerous myth. The truth is that if we wish to develop children's thinking and understanding we must structure their work in accordance with the features which are immanent in the activities of thinking and coming to understand themselves, rather than some separated and predefined end-product. Our stance must be to think of opportunities given rather than precise outcomes to be achieved. (Which is not, of course, to deny that we may want to check what has been achieved, insofar as this is possible. This issue is taken up in the next chapter.)

This approach to the structuring of learning which focuses on the quality of experience offered is very much in keeping with what was said concerning the application for the teacher of the constituents of understanding summarized at the end of the previous chapter. In this broader context it would provoke planning which centred around complementary questions concerning the extent to which children are given opportunities to, say, empathize, be affected by, appreciate underlying motives, apply public classificatory rules, patterns and webs of argument, etc. It would place at the centre of our planning the question: In which contexts should we be attempting to be building such qualities into children's learning experiences, and how can this be married with the intrinsically more closed principles of structure? Somehow in our planning, the latter have to be restored to the position of being potentially enriching of authentic understanding, i.e. as desirable *possibilities*, rather than as a potentially deadening straitjacket of prescribed outcomes.

Openness and the National Curriculum

We must now consider the last of our three questions: to what degree is it possible to structure learning in this way in the context of the National Curriculum? Clearly this will vary to some degree across foundation subject areas. As one might expect, there would seem to be generally more scope in areas such as English than in Mathematics and Science. In a moment I will consider this in more detail, but first it is important to reassert a general point made in Part One concerning the relationship of teachers to the National Curriculum: they have an interpretive and formative role to play. Strictly speaking the National Curriculum is an abstract set of formal legal requirements which have to be interpreted in a wide range of differing practical situations to the benefit of the children concerned. The helpfulness of the framework provided by the National Curriculum is not a given – it cannot be – but is to be *discovered* and *developed* in the contexts in which it is applied. It is therefore a framework which will need to evolve in the light of professional response. If quality of development in children's thinking and understanding is to be enhanced, teachers will need to continue to exercise a significant degree of autonomy in terms of how they implement it. In particular they will need to mediate it in a way that mitigates the possible negative effects of the extensive and detailed compulsory elements on the quality of children's understanding, as I have previously tried to explain and defend it. Interestingly, as we shall see, certain aspects of the National Curriculum – particularly elements in the various Programmes of Study – seem to be very much in harmony with this, but there can be little doubt that the strong pressures in the opposite direction will require teachers to be very active in seeking opportunities to organize in appropriate experiences.

By way of example, let us now consider some of the statements of attainment in Science to see what scope there is for structuring children's learning in the way we have been discussing. One thing that becomes rapidly clear is that, far from this possibility being prohibited, it is to some degree *required*. For example, consider the following statements of attainment taken from Levels 1–5 of Attainment target 1: Scientific investigation:[4]

- observe familiar materials and events
- ask questions such as 'How . . .?' Why . . .?' and 'What will happen if . . .?', suggest ideas and make predictions
- make a series of related observations

- suggest questions, ideas and predictions, based on everyday experience, which can be tested
- carry out a fair test in which they select and use appropriate instruments to measure quantities such as volume and temperature
- draw conclusions which link patterns in observations, or results to the original question, prediction or idea
- evaluate the validity of their conclusions by considering different interpretations of their experimental evidence

Such a list could clearly be construed as a detailed set of procedural principles, and reference to the accompanying Programme of Study, which suggests that such activities should 'develop investigative skills and understanding of science through activities which . . . encourage the raising and answering of questions . . . are within everyday experience and provide opportunities to explore, with increasing precision . . .', only encourages such an interpretation.

It is true, of course, that other attainment targets are more content specific, so we find under 'Attainment target 2: Life and living processes', such objectives as 'know that plants and animals need certain conditions to sustain life', and under 'Attainment target 3: Materials and their properties': 'know that heating and cooling everyday materials can cause them to melt or solidify', and 'know that the combustion of fuel releases energy and produces waste gases'. But even here, there seems to be a considerable degree of openness with regard to the detailed experiences that children may have which could develop such knowledge. The main point to be taken from this, I think, is that in theory many (though maybe not all) statements of attainment have in some degree the potential to be achieved in ways consistent with the approach to structuring children's learning which has been advocated in this chapter. There is *some* space for this, and even in the area of Mathematics[5] we find such promising statements as 'Pupils should choose and make use of knowledge skills and understanding . . . in practical tasks, in real-life problems and to investigate within mathematics itself', though the statements of attainment for 'Attainment target 2: Number', for example, tend to be more content-specific and hierarchically ordered than in Science.

In the light of this assessment of the situation, it seems to me that we are left with two crucial questions with regard to the future of 'open' principles of structure within the National Curriculum. The first is whether teachers believe sufficiently in their value to seriously pursue them, given that the various elements of negotiation with children which they entail will, on the face of it, place extra demands upon them. The second question is whether they will receive the necessary help in terms of encouragement, time, and resources to support them in the attempt.

These questions are particularly pressing in a situation where teachers are having to cope with rapid change, and the sheer range of demands which comprise the nine foundation subjects (plus RE) with their myriad detailed statements of attainment, and additional cross-curricular themes. It is not so much that any single element within the National Curriculum framework is inherently hostile to the approach to structuring advocated here – though there undoubtedly *is* a tension over the issue of pre-specification as such – but that the cumulative requirements of planning for, teaching, monitoring and reporting such an extensive and detailed set of objectives will preoccupy teachers to such an extent that there is a real danger of the concerns of children simply disappearing from view. But perhaps of equal significance, the approach of teachers to structuring children's learning in this context is likely to be strongly influenced by the forms of assessment in terms of which their own and their children's performance is to be judged. To this complex issue, I will now turn.

NOTES AND REFERENCES

1 Thus over recent years researchers have identified differences in terms of convergers/divergers, focusers/scanners, holists/serialists, analytic/global, reflective/impulsive. See Conner (1988) for a useful survey of such findings.
2 See Stenhouse (1971).
3 See Stenhouse (1975), Ch. 7. Also there is an interesting discussion of some closely related issues in Bridges (1988), Chs 1, 2 and 7.
4 DES (1991a).
5 DES (1991b).

CHAPTER 13

Assessing Children's Thinking and Understanding

Some basic considerations

In Chapter 2 the point was made that the very notions of 'education' and 'development' contain within them the idea of a person's achieving some new, higher, standard in their thinking and understanding. That is to say, teaching in this context is concerned with the bringing about of some kind of desirable change in children. If this is so, it would seem to follow that anyone seriously involved in such teaching must be committed to the idea of assessment in some form or other, for how else could they judge whether this desirable change is taking place, and therefore the extent to which their teaching is working? This is not of course to deny that some important educational changes take place that do not necessarily manifest themselves in a form directly observable by the teacher. A child's deeper understanding of an issue, a piece of literature or music, may find no expression that can be identified and used as a measure by an observer. Here assessment must be of the quality of the procedures, materials, interaction, that are provided to *facilitate* change rather than the change itself. But one way or another assessment seems to be absolutely necessary if we are to discover whether our teaching is doing, or is likely to be doing, any good, and what improvements should be sought. This being so, the main question is not *whether* to assess – since to seriously engage in the activity of teaching at all seems to require it – but *how* to assess. What form(s) should assessment take in particular circumstances?

The aspect of assessment which focuses on the educational potential of a situation through an analysis of the quality of experience being provided for a child has in fact been discussed in the previous chapter where the possibilities of structuring children's thinking through principles of procedure were explored. Such principles, along with others relating to the nature of the materials being used and the resources provided, would provide a set of criteria for analysing and evaluating such educational potential – as would the components of understanding offered at the end of Chapter 11. This general perspective will be taken a little further in the final chapter on teaching as poetry. In the present discussion, I will focus on the issue of attempting to assess what children *have* learnt as against what they may have had the opportunity to learn. That is to say I will be addressing the following fundamental question for educational assessment: *What conditions provide the maximum opportunity for overt responses which are a true expression of a child's thinking and understanding?* Unfortunately, this is not always the question which leads assessment today. How to achieve objectivity, fair comparisons, convenience of marking, and ease of producing numerical grades often come higher up the list. But such a question must nonetheless remain central to any notion of validity.

Now clearly, how one sets about answering this question will depend upon one's underlying philosophy of education – what one values and what precisely one is trying to achieve as a teacher. And it will be against this backcloth that three more precise questions present themselves with regard to selecting a means of assessment in any particular context:

(1) Precisely what is it that you wish to assess?
  – what is its nature?
  – of what is it comprised?
(2) Precisely why do you wish to assess it?
  – what advantages do you hope to gain?
  – to what purpose will the assessment be put?
  – what will hang on it?
(3) What are the possible side-effects, intended and otherwise?
  – are there any dangers/reservations about making this assessment, and in this form, in terms of possible effects on other aspects of what one values educationally? For example, how will it affect children's motivation, attitudes, and the relative status of those things that can be/are assessed as against those things that can't be or are not?

In sum, the appropriate form of an assessment must depend upon consideration of the nature of the thing to be assessed, your purpose in doing so, and its possible broader consequences. In the light of these very basic points about assessment in general, I will now turn to the more specific issue of assessing the development of children's thinking in the climate of expectations created by the National Curriculum.

Assessing authentic–rational and poetic thinking

I have tried in this book to describe two kinds of thinking, and a third dimension of thinking which is in interplay with them. Since these accounts constitute an answer to the first of the three basic questions listed above, it may be helpful at this point to recap. Basically, I have tried to make a distinction between rational–calculative thinking and poetic thinking, each with its own project with regard to reality: the former seeking to master reality by interpreting it through an imposed system of defining categories which standardize things and thus make them manageable; the latter seeking to simply reveal reality through a direct relationship with things themselves which is receptive to their uniqueness. The one gains organizational and explanatory power by levelling off the particular and seeing it as an instance of something more general, as, say, when we see a person as being of a certain 'personality type' or exemplifying a certain cultural background. The other gains depth of felt response by involving itself in the here and now and thus apprehends universals concerning, for example, the human situation, that are immanent in the present as, say, when we are moved by a particular individual's courage or compassion, fear or jealousy, which deepens our understanding of what these things can mean.

The third dimension comes into play as follows. Insofar as rational–calculative thinking emphasizes the impersonal aspects of thinking in the form of public conventions and standards, it holds within it the danger of the individual overlooking his or her *own* understanding of the ideas and procedures he or she may be employing: their subjective weight. Thus there is a need to encourage what I have termed authenticity of thought, wherein individuals make what they have learnt their own by coming to feel its value in the context of their own real concerns, i.e. *concerns, for the expression of which they accept personal responsibility.*

In this way the use of rational thinking can become self-expressive, and when the subjective and objective elements are so combined we have what I have dubbed authentic-rational thinking.

Poetic thinking, on the other hand, as I have characterized it, necessarily involves self-expression within itself, for at its heart lies a relationship of direct personal response of the individual to the thing being thought. The individual is attuned to what things themselves invoke in him with no further end in view, though it is important to note that this is not to deny that such attunement may well affect his understanding of, and attitude towards, many other things. For example, one's more poetic apprehension of a situation may condition one's stance towards rational interpretations and explanations of it, and affect the way one weighs alternative reasons and evaluations in relation to it, as, say, when the sublime subtlety of a wild flower in the grass may disturb an existing predisposition to see life as merely the mechanical product of blind evolutionary forces or as to be devoted to the pursuit of a higher standard of living, above all else.

Having thus sharpened our focus in terms of the broad modes of thinking we are trying to assess, let us firstly look in more detail at the case of authentic-rational thinking. Examination of this view of what it is to think and understand has made it clear that what we should be trying to assess is the extent to which children have acquired publicly shared concepts and procedures, made sense of them in terms of their own existence and can apply them in their experience. And in providing this focus, it draws our attention to two questions central to the idea of assessing the development of children's thinking:

1. What counts as having learnt a concept?
2. Is there any necessary order in which concepts have to be learnt?

There is much that could be said on both of these issues, but previous discussion has drawn attention to the following important points. Firstly, the rationalist notion of webs of concepts emphasizes that concepts do not exist in isolation, and that they derive their meaning from the human activity in which they are embedded, and which they help to articulate. Thus, the answer to the first question is that we must think less in terms of the learning of individual concepts and more in terms of initiation into conceptual networks and the practices in which they are embedded. From this it would seem to follow that the degree of success here can only be displayed in how someone organizes experience over a relatively broad front and in a meaningful context.

Now if this is so, and we recall the point underlined by the notion of authenticity concerning the need for a psychological rather than a logical point of reference for the sequencing of learning, a second important consideration arises. It may well turn out to be the case that any attempt to tightly pre-specify the course of learning for an individual will be counter-productive. We saw that 'straight' rationalism tended to focus on the public dimension of meaning. But if we allow credence to the view that understanding has a personal dimension that is a function of the particular individual's present concerns and conception of a situation, then effective learning will require to take a direction that is significantly shaped by the learner. Thus the route that an individual will follow cannot be prescribed, but will result from an on-going process of negotiation within a situation. If this is the case, there are some important consequences for the assessment of authentic–rational thinking.

Firstly, assessment will need to be *retrospective* in character. While it may be possible to pre-specify the area to be assessed in general terms, e.g. by indicating some of the central concepts and procedures that characterize it, selection of precise elements and levels can only be made with hindsight. That is to say, assessment must take as its point of reference an evaluation of the potential of the experience that *the children actually had*. This is not, of course, to say that it should simply replicate such experience – far from it. We should recall here the point made by Wittgenstein (Chapter 5) that understanding is only demonstrated when a person shows that they can apply what they have learnt in situations which are new to them. The point is that it is only in the light of such a looking back that we can establish fitting criteria for testing what has been learnt, for the detailed course of the child's learning cannot be predicted if he or she is active in shaping it. Thus while assessment may rightly take place within the context of a broad framework of general attainment targets, it must be designed to *reflect* the real learning experience and not tightly *prescribe* it.

Secondly, it would seem to follow that assessment should aim to take a form in which children perform in situations which are as 'natural' as possible. That is to say, it should have as its focus episodes which have a psychological continuity with the children's own concerns and conceptions. Quality of learning is most trenchantly measured according to the degree of novelty of the situation in which it is having to be applied, and the opportunities it offers for application of the web of concepts (rather than one member) *in a context that has intrinsic meaning to the learner.* This last consideration is perhaps particularly endangered when heavy emphasis is placed on attempting to standardize assessments.

Thirdly, as Christian Schiller once claimed, assessment should be of children 'in the round'.[1] The ability to give a formal statement of the criteria for a concept, to match terms with definitions, and to recognize instances in a prescribed situation, says little concerning the extent to which children have made such an aspect of understanding their own. To judge this authentic quality, we need to take the trouble to see how it has become incorporated into their normal way of going about things – how it affects their outlook and their lives. To what extent do they employ *out of their own volition* concepts and procedures they have learnt? That is to say, we need to observe what difference their learning makes to them as individuals. As we have noted, developing children's thinking is not a purely cognitive matter, it is centrally concerned with attitudes and dispositions. Assessment which does not reflect this is of very limited value, for it tells us nothing about the meaning of what has been learnt for the learner. These considerations, taken together, seem to argue powerfully for forms of assessment which are either illuminative descriptions of the child's developing way of identifying and dealing with problems, or more standardized test material which has become an integrated part of the child's on-going work.

Let us now consider some of the implications for the assessment of the development of children's thinking, which our consideration of the poetic raises. Clearly, it would seem to reassert the great importance of aspects of thought which are not readily developed in a tightly structured way, and which are notoriously difficult to assess objectively. Poetic thinking demands a kind of personal involvement which cannot be standardized and pre-specified because, in essence, it consists of forms of unique subjective response which require openness and freedom. And it follows from this that it requires a teaching relationship which is *itself* poetic in character, such that what an individual brings to the situation is respected in its own right and is developed in ways that maintain its inner integrity. But, as I have previously been at pains to emphasize, this is far from saying that whatever response a child may have is simply to be indulged (and therefore likely ossified and stultified): it has to be challenged and deepened, but in ways which are an empathetic response to that individual, and which we therefore cannot map out in advance. It is not that there are *no* standards in this area, but rather that they are of a qualitatively different kind to those employed in rational–calculative thinking.

Let me illustrate this, and its consequences for assessment, by using a familiar example. Consider the development of, say, a child's creative writing. Clearly this depends upon the acquisition of many basic social conventions to do with the shared meanings of words, grammar, symbolism etc., whose use can be assessed to some extent 'objectively'. But also, we feel able to make judgements concerning the quality of such a piece of writing which go beyond the correct application of conventions, yet are not thereby purely arbitrary. Here, such standards as we employ are themselves subservient to something more fundamental, namely the inner integrity of the piece – the extent that it reveals the felt reality of its subject. That is to say conventions are employed, and standards are applied, in the service of expressing and invoking a fresh and direct response to things themselves. It is this relationship of open awareness which is the final point of reference, the ultimate standard. And this itself is infinite in terms of its variation, and cannot be standardized. Thus truly creative writing is always a manifestation of a vital and receptive involvement with a situation or thing, and it is for this reason that a piece displaying perfect grammar and syntax, richness and breadth of vocabulary, might come across as hackneyed and somehow secondhand when compared with another piece consisting of a few simple lines.

And what is true here, is, I suggest, as true in analogous ways for quality of thinking in many other areas of the arts and humanities, and also, importantly, in the area of interpersonal relationships. Ultimately, there are no recipes, no prescriptions, there is no 'method' or definitive set of separate 'skills', and therefore no pre-specifiable outcomes in terms of which the quality of poetic thinking can be mechanically measured. On the contrary, those who would assess such thinking must themselves be prepared to enter into the experience – the relationship – in which it occurred. To assess the development of children's poetic thinking, then, must involve an empathetic relationship with the individual child him- or herself, for what we are attempting to evaluate is genuineness of self-expression, where this latter term denotes not a self-centred indulgence, but a demanding and creative relationship with things – a receptive, and therefore genuinely personal response.

In having our attention drawn to the empathetic and receptive role of the teacher in developing a child's poetic thinking, and therefore to the openness and unpredictability of a learning episode, it can be seen that any 'test' of such thinking needs to be modifiable by the participants during the progress of the test. Only through a significant degree of such *interaction* with the form of assessment can the pupil's own understanding come into play in such a way as to allow on-going psychological continuity and the demonstration of her capacity for creative response to the situation (which itself becomes modified in line with the pupil's evolving conception of it).

Similarly, it will be highly desirable for the teacher, through oral and other contributions, to be able to elicit fuller and deeper responses from pupils and to be able to modify the test so as to allow it to build upon these and thus reflect more accurately the quality of understanding of the children. This facility, then, is not merely to safeguard against inaccuracy of assessment arising from ambiguities of interpretation of the test (where some depth and creativity of response is sought, there is always likely to be a danger of this), it is required to enable fullness of response which may indicate the extent to which the pupil has made what she

171

knows her own, and how it has affected her outlook to a situation. From the perspective of those preoccupied with the kind of 'objectivity' which seeks to reduce things to the measurable and easily comparable, such action by the teacher would look quite out of place. From the poetic perspective, however, to rule out opportunities to explore and reveal such quality of understanding on the grounds that it was not the originally specified focus of the test, would itself seem to amount to arbitrariness of a pretty high order.

But now, if, because of its open and highly subjective nature, it is clear that there cannot be a narrow and tightly pre-specified set of standards to refer to with regard to poetic thinking, the question arises as to how we are to assess children's progress here at all. What seems to be needed is an understanding of a wide range of loose-textured *potential* criteria which can be called into play as appropriate to evaluate a particular response – to be interpreted in ways that reflect the inner integrity of that response. Such potential criteria would include degree of vitality, perceptiveness, sensitivity, freshness of expression, aptness, engagement, empathy with subject, atmosphere, integrity, depth of meaning, revealment, self-expressiveness, imaginativeness, effectiveness of imagery and symbolism, etc. As previously mentioned, such evaluation will largely rest on an intuitive entering into the work and would need to be accompanied by the pupil's own view of his or her achievement. In the same way as one can often only convey the quality of a poem or novel by quoting extracts because its quality lies precisely in its particular and unique expression, which is therefore not quantifiable in any straightforward sense of that term, so it would seem that progress in the development of children's poetic thinking will be best conveyed by the collection of selected examples of children's responses together with appropriate scene-setting and evaluative comments, which could then be compared over a period of time. Judgements might then be made which involve some degree of re-entry into the situation which provoked the pupil's response.

Résumé: criteria of assessment

Let me now summarize the view of assessment we have reached. In the light of the distinctions I have made, I have suggested a number of features of forms of assessment which would genuinely reflect the development of children's thinking would possess. From a consideration of authentic–rational thinking arose the importance of assessments which assess understanding of webs of concepts, are retrospective in orientation, hold psychological continuity and intrinsic meaning for the learner, and reflect the way what has been learnt affects the learner's own way of dealing with problems in their everyday living. Our exploration of the notion of poetic thinking has suggested the desirability of assessments which are open-ended, modifiable by the participants through their evolving interaction with a situation, and involve the empathetic sharing of particular responses by the assessor. It is important to note that although these latter requirements arose out of a consideration of the nature of poetic thinking, there is a highly significant sense in which they are appropriate to the assessment of *any* thinking, since if we wish to achieve assessment in any full *educational* sense we must be significantly concerned with the progress of unique individuals in their own understanding of what they have learnt. This need for genuine receptiveness to the individual child means that educational assessment itself, therefore, has an integral poetic dimension. Once acknowledged, this clearly has huge implications – most of which run counter to the current drive to produce standardized scores. Finally, such considerations taken together have suggested that assessment will be most illuminating where:

1. it arises out of an on-going learning situation and is an integral part of it;
2. it draws on real concerns of the participants;
3. it parallels but does not simply repeat previous classroom situations and tasks.

Assessment and the National Curriculum

Much of the current concern in primary schools with assessment of pupil performance has been provoked by the demands for monitoring the achievement of National Curriculum attainment targets and more detailed statements of attainment. It is difficult to say very much concerning the specific requirements of the

National Curriculum in this regard at present as they are in a state of flux, both in terms of their scope and their form. For example, at the time of writing an increase in the proportion of 'pencil and paper' tests is being advocated on the grounds of ease of administration and economy of resources. However, the underlying principles which were to guide assessment in the National Curriculum are set out in the report of the Task Group on Assessment and Testing (TGAT),[2] with examples of what are considered to be suitable tests described in Appendices D and E of that report. Since one of the central aspirations of the TGAT report was to produce a framework for testing that would avoid many of the well-known pitfalls in the area, I intend, in the final part of this chapter, to look at these proposals from the point of view of the criteria for assessment which have emerged from our discussion. The likely effects of any future deviation from the TGAT proposals, particularly in the direction of streamlining tests for ease of administration, will, I think, become very apparent in the course of this discussion.

The first thing to note is that it is clear (and hardly surprising) that the tests described in the TGAT report focus on rational–calculative thinking in its various forms. All the tests, when they rise above the level of basic comprehension, set problems to be solved, albeit of a wide variety and involving differing modes of 'presentation', 'operation' and 'response'. Indeed, in the school context, perhaps the very notion of a 'test' implies this calculative orientation towards the nature of thinking, since it commonly denotes evaluation in accordance with a carefully pre-specified set of public standards. Be this as it may, this is clearly the case with the 'standard assessment tasks' – SATs – with which the report is concerned, for as their name suggests, their purpose is to provide common points of reference in the moderation of more informal on-going assessments made by individual teachers.

If we consider such tests in the light of the criteria of adequacy previously set out, one welcome feature of many of those described in the report is the importance attached to group discussion of the problem set. This has two virtues from the point of the view expressed in this chapter. Firstly, it enhances the possibility of the pupil's understanding of the web of interrelated concepts being brought to bear in working towards a solution;

secondly, it may facilitate some degree of psychological continuity (albeit, in a weak sense) through calling into play previous experience and concerns. Both of these considerations are likely to be best accommodated in what TGAT refers to as 'integrating tests' (exemplified in Appendix D), which consist of a series of evolving tasks (e.g. investigations into the properties and uses of various materials) which could form an integrated part of the on-going work of a class.

Again, psychological continuity and intrinsic meaning for the pupil could well be retained to some degree in tests whose specific content consisted of subject matter and situations which are commonly of interest to the group being tested, e.g. perhaps 'animals' for younger children, though better still would be a use of SATs which maintained a fairly constant form in terms of skills and underlying concepts involved, but which allowed of some substitution of differing specific subject content – to be determined by the teacher in the light of her knowledge of the concerns of her pupils. Finally, from the point of view of appropriate testing of rational–calculative thinking, the notion strongly emphasized in the TGAT report, of teachers being able to select from a bank of SATs, might allow some scope for the criteria of attainment being selected retrospectively, so as to reflect the actual learning experiences of a particular group of children, though clearly this will largely depend on the range and imaginativeness of the tests 'stocked'.

The above features, then, are generally to be welcomed, and some of my comments intimate ways in which considerations raised by the notion of poetic thinking have a bearing upon, and could lead to exploring, ways in which pupil participation in the assessment could become more interactive. But so far I have only considered the report's recommendations for assessment from the point of view of rational–calculative thinking, and the poetic role of the teacher in facilitating its authentic development. Regarding the assessment of the development of poetic thinking *per se*, clearly the notion of a standard assessment task would need to become even more tenuous, and is perhaps best abandoned altogether. If this is in fact the view of those who compiled the TGAT report, it is to be applauded – as long as, that is, this does not carry with it the practical consequence that the development of children's poetic thinking becomes viewed as being of lesser importance, so that assessment of progress in this area need not receive proper attention. It may be that here there will be a pressing need for teachers to engage in a certain amount of 'artful subversion' if the place in the curriculum of aspects of education that are not susceptible to standardized measurement is not to be undermined.

By way of conclusion I would like to make a final comment on the implications of taking assessment of children's thinking seriously. It is only too evident that if we really wish to assess the development and quality of children's thinking in either its rational–calculative or poetic modes, this is likely to be time-consuming, require sensitive and skilled judgement, and will often not produce results that are straightforward and easily understood by people external to the teaching situation. Real assessment of children's thinking will rarely produce a simple set of grades and will be seriously corrupted by any attempts to impose such reductionism. Now these features are not criticisms of such assessment, but criticisms of some of the purposes to which some people have seemed to wish to put assessment (e.g. as a cheap and public way of maintaining standards, making easy comparisons of quality of education between teachers, or schools, etc.). Both the large resource implications, and the strict limitations on the extent to which assessment of children's thinking can be used as a yardstick for purposes external to the educative process itself, must be honestly acknowledged if what should be a spur to more effective teaching is not to be turned into a distorting and vacuous charade.

NOTES AND REFERENCES

1   Schiller (1946).
2   DES (1988).

CHAPTER 14

Teaching as Poetry

Towards a philosophy of teaching

In this final chapter I would like to try to draw together a number of points which have emerged in a rather piecemeal way during the course of this book, but which seem to me to provide a coherent philosophy for teaching with regard to the development of children's authentic thinking and understanding. It may be recalled that in a number of places I have made mention of the idea of there being a poetic element to the teacher–pupil relationship in which authenticity of thought is being encouraged. Similarly, the notion arose again in the context of assessment which seriously seeks to reflect an individual's true understanding. What lies at the bottom of these suggestions is a claim which is fundamental to poetic thinking itself, namely, that to reveal an individual in its uniqueness one's stance has to be basically receptive–responsive, rather than manipulative. One has, in the first instance, to listen non-judgementally, i.e. non-evaluatively, if the thing or person is to be self-expressive, and thus authentically known.

But, as we have noted, teaching is not merely a matter of being receptive to what is there, it is concerned with the bringing about of desirable change, i.e. development. That is to say it is a form of *building* – a form of building which respects the integrity of the self of the learner and the nature of the things to be learnt. It has to be somehow both accepting and demanding. I have previously used the term 'empathetic challenging' to denote this idea. I would now like to say a little more about it.[1]

In many approaches to education, and to life in a more general sense, there has been a tendency to reflect an enduring philosophical dichotomy between the objective and the subjective, public rationality and personal feeling or intuition, what is present 'in reality' and what is present 'in the mind'. This is in part, the history of a dialectic between classicism and romanticism which, in turn, has underpinned the educational debate between traditionalism and progressivism – the one taking the structure of objective, public, knowledge as its main point of reference, the other taking the consciousness of the learner as its main point of reference. While there have been varying attempts to overcome this dualism, in many cases they have not really succeeded because they have either fallen back into it, or attempted to reduce everything to one or other pole, as in the cases of philosophical materialism and idealism. How then, does the idea of poetic thinking help in this regard? How can it help to restore a proper balance between the subjective and objective poles in the development of thinking and understanding? It does this, I suggest, by encouraging us to focus not on the poles, but on *the relationship between them*. That is to say it predisposes us to take as primal the relationship between teacher and learner, and learner and what is to be learnt.

It is the quality of these relationships, which in effect form a triad, that should be the central concern of those who wish to promote the development of children's thinking. The elements of this triadic relationship are nothing independently of it, they are sustained only insofar as they remain expressions of it. Existentially, there is no teacher in the absence of a learner and something to teach; there is no learner in the absence of something to be learnt; and there is nothing to be learnt in the absence of a learner. Put more generally, and starkly, things have no significance in the absence of consciousness and consciousness has no existence in the absence of things, for it precisely consists in its relating to them.

Our starting point for a theory of effective learning has to be the actual experience of learning. Experience is the name we give to the relationship between consciousness and things in their mutual reaching towards each other. That's what they are: a mutual reaching out, elements-in-relationship. When we are struck, say, by the brilliance of a colour, the heaviness of a rock, the solidity of a building, the softness of a fabric, the appeal of a story, the magnificence of the heavens or a mountain, the elegance of a proof or theory – all these qualities of things, *that make them what they are*, are neither simply human projections

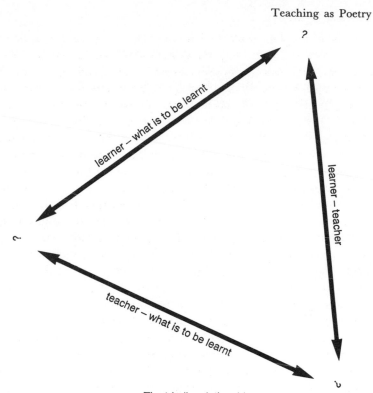

The triadic relationship

Figure 14.1 The triadic relationship.

(there's a clear sense in which we regard them as belonging to the things themselves), nor simply independently existing properties (they exist as such – stand forth – only in being apprehended by consciousness). They are expressions of the relationship in which consciousness and things are rooted. From this perspective the essential relationship in which the activities of teaching are rooted can be represented diagrammatically as above.

The central point here is that precisely what is to be learnt, what it is to be a learner, what it is to be a teacher, are not separately pre-specifiable, but emerge from the particular situations created by a set of reciprocal relationships. This is clearly

179

at odds with those current approaches to curriculum planning which increasingly demand that all such things are carefully defined in advance. Clarity of purpose is thereby conflated with pre-set standards and goals, which run across and obscure the demands of real learning. Here again, the drive to make everything transparent, tangible, and thus more straightforwardly accountable, leaves the realities of things themselves covered over and untouched. Standards are 'met' or 'not met', goals are 'achieved' or 'failed in', and the authentic life of the mind is by-passed, or worse, destroyed.

If, on the other hand, we take the quality of the triadic relationship as primal, we have to look at the quality of its openness, and the extent to which it is free to follow its own path and establish its own goals in the light of its own constantly evolving needs. From this perspective, facilitating learning requires the teacher to 'listen' for what is incipiently there in the consciousness of the pupil: the questions and possibilities that his or her present thinking inherently holds within itself – and to challenge him or her to acknowledge and pursue them. To do this the teacher must also 'listen' to what things themselves (including, of course, human culture and its artefacts) have to offer so that she can put the pupil in the way of new experiences which may contribute to a deeper and broader understanding. Thus she is attempting to focus on neither the individual child in isolation, nor some pre-specified piece of knowledge, but *the engagement of children in whatever seriously occupies them* – their way of relating in a situation, and what is provoking it. In the light of her own knowledge and experience, she can thus try to help the child to identify and explore what calls to be thought in this situation and to give the space for this to occur.

Since I am here advocating a stance towards teaching which takes as a central point of reference the quality of particular learning situations, it is difficult to be very specific about exactly how the teacher should operate. There must be considerable scope for professional judgement here. Indeed, this is of the essence. But there are some features of this stance which can be sketched out a little more fully. For example, it is clear that discussion will be an important element of this approach and that the sorts of questions asked in order to stimulate it would need to be of a certain

character – essentially focusing on the quality of relationship between learner and what he or she is learning rather than assumed
end-products that the teacher may have in mind. They would
therefore tend to be of the following variety:

How are you getting on?
What do you feel about this?
What made you decide to do it this way?
How do you know?
What else did you think of?
What was the hardest thing here?
How could you deal with this problem?

Such an approach to questioning has been termed 'person-
centred' because it focuses on the learner's actions, ideas and
problems rather than the subject matter as such, and provokes
the child to articulate how he is engaging with the situation, to
justify his ideas, to reflect on problems.[2] But it seems to me that
it is important for the teacher to further challenge thinking
by on occasion offering something of her own response to the
situation – pointing out features that strike her as significant, but
again, *in relation to aspirations expressed by the learners* in their own
engagement with the material rather than in terms she simply
wishes to impose on them. Through this she would be able to help
children to become aware of more than what may be immediately
apparent to them – in terms, for example, of the fullness of what
is present, what it could be taken to exemplify, relationships to
other things they have learnt, and of possible alternatives through
offering the views and experiences of others who have been
engaged in a similar enterprise (drawn perhaps from the history
of the discipline, or work that other children in the class have
done). In other words, she will attempt to bring out some of the
further possibilities of the situation, a sense of the fuller potential
that the engagement holds within it and the often communal
nature of enquiry.

Of course a crucial aspect of all this will be the spirit in
which it is done, and *received*. It needs to occur in a spirit of
offering rather than prescribing – and offering out of a sense of
what things themselves demand rather than purely out of the
teacher's personal preferences or anxiety to cover some externally

pre-specified content. That is to say, there is an important impersonal element to the relationship in which the teacher's contributions arise out of her sense of something other than herself: her
sense of things themselves in the traditions in which they have
achieved their significance. Thus such interaction is not about
indulging the egos of those involved, but about getting closer to
truth, an understanding rooted in responsiveness and responsibility to what is there. Harking back to the distinction made
when we were discussing authenticity: self-referencing, yes, but
not self-centredness – on the part, now, of both pupil and
teacher.

This last reference brings back to mind another important
aspect of the interaction between teacher and child: the need to
wean the child away from 'crowd' responses. In the educational
situation, the triadic relationship I have introduced into our
discussion in this chapter offers, I think, an important perspective
on this issue. It begins to make it clear that 'personal meaning',
'subjective weight', is not purely a personal matter; it occurs as
part of a larger relationship in which things themselves and the
views and experiences of other people are also involved. Thus in
helping the child to identify and discover his deeper concerns –
ones for which he feels a sense of responsibility – the teacher's
role is precisely this: to point him at things which he can recognize
as relevant. But not simply in the sense of what satisfies
immediate whim or curiosity, rather in the sense of what makes
a *call* upon him, what *demands* something from him, what he feels
(however embryonically) *needs* a response arising from his own
sense of the nature of the thing he is dealing with.

And, clearly, the role of the teacher here in helping the child
explore his concerns is not to jump in for him and hand him back
his problems ready sorted out. By taking over someone's concerns
and problems in this way one throws them out of position,
disengages them, leaving them to mentally 'free wheel' aimlessly
while at the same time becoming dependent and dominated.
Rather, by attending to the enterprise itself, one helps the child
to understand himself *in* his care, in his 'relationship-with', to
grasp it more adequately and work towards his own provisional
solutions. To feel for himself, say, how a new piece of evidence
calls for the reappraisal of a theory, how a poem calls to him to

view himself or some aspect of the world afresh, or how some deeper apprehension of the moral dimension of a situation calls upon him to respond in a fuller way. Thus he becomes liberated through being more deeply situated in his relationship with things – through the enhancement of his ability to receive and to respond. In this way he is given *positive* freedom rather than the negative freedom of thoughtless non-intervention that has become associated with some forms of child-centred education.

In this way, too, teaching can become what one might term a form of 'poetic building' – a form of building which expresses respect and harmony rather than manipulation and imposition. Such teaching would have as its central concern the organic growth of individuals in their own relationship with the world, their sense of mutual belonging, and not to process them in accordance with norms that are external to them. Yet, nonetheless, it would be concerned, too, to help them feel the call for themselves of what is there to be thought, to sense the harmonies and the conflicts. This at least would be the ideal. But, of course, it is well known that teachers do not operate in circumstances where pure ideals flourish. So what is the point of all this in real terms? How can it make a difference to anything?

Ideals and practice

It would be disingenuous to advocate such an educational ideal as teaching as poetic building without discussing some of the obvious practical issues that it throws up in schools as we presently know them. It is probably true that we are entering a period when the formal constraints on teachers' freedom and the explicit demands on an individual teacher's time and energy are greater than at any period since the turn of the century, when the system of payment by results was in operation. How, then, is the ideal of poetic openness and building to find practical expression in such a situation? Before attempting to answer this question directly I must make clear some important points concerning the nature and function of educational ideals.

The first, and central, point is that it is not in the nature of an ideal that it be perfectly attainable: it is not the function of an ideal to provide a fulfilable objective, but rather to provide a sense of direction and underlying purpose. An ideal indicates a path one may wish to tread rather than a destination to have arrived at. Two things follow from this. The first is that the extent to which anyone achieves an ideal is always a matter of *degree*. Sometimes one may not get very far, but the assumption would be that it is better to get some of the way than none of the way. The second is that one measures success not simply in terms of how far one gets, but equally in terms of the conditions under which one is 'travelling'. In uncongenial circumstances to travel a short way deserves to be a source of considerable satisfaction. Many teachers have a well-developed sense of what counts as a real achievement for a particular child which takes proper account of where that child is starting from. This is precisely the stance that needs to be adopted in gauging their own performance in terms of an ideal. It is lack of realism in the *application* of ideals, rather than lack of realism in the ideals themselves, that leads to frustration and disillusionment in practice, which in turn can so easily form a (false) basis for dismissing them out of hand.

A second very important point is that it is not the function of ideals to provide recipes for teaching. How, in detail, one is to teach cannot be simply determined by an ideal, which by its very nature exists independently of a particular teaching situation. Indeed, as was noted in Chapter 3, there are simply too many context-dependent variables in teaching to permit the successful use of *any* off-the-shelf recipes. An ideal provides a sense of purpose which is *one* consideration to be brought into play along with many others in making practical decisions about what to do. That is to say, how an ideal is to find expression in a particular teaching context – the extent to which it should even come into play – is a matter of the creative response of the teacher involved. It will need to take account not only of such objective features of a situation as resources and externally imposed constraints, but the disposition of the children and the teacher's own strengths and weaknesses and level of confidence. There are going to be many compromises, and the thing to be aimed for is to strike the best compromise under the circumstances. Teachers never start with a blank slate upon which to simply etch highflown ideals, they always take up an on-going situation to which they often have to respond in a piecemeal way over a period of time. Indeed, sometimes the most effective way of working towards an ideal is to use it as a criterion in terms of which one evaluates past and present practice and in the light of this propose small but significant changes to try in future. That is to say, ideals are often best pursued through gradual evolution rather than revolution, and in this process they may themselves become reinterpreted and refined in the light of new experiences and deeper understanding of particular contexts that the attempt to express them can itself provoke. For to seek to actively promote an ideal can lead us to ask new questions, see existing practice from new perspectives, reconceptualize old problems and become alert to new solutions.[3]

Practical organization

Given this understanding of the way an ideal functions in terms of practical decision-making, let us now turn to the issue of planning and organizing for teaching as poetic building. The first thing that I should like to emphasize is that there is nothing particularly esoteric involved here. Focusing on the quality of the openness in the triadic relationship between teacher, learner, and that which is to be learnt, broadly requires three things:

1.   To establish as clearly as possible what is, initially at least, negotiable and what is non-negotiable about one's situation. In a context of increasing formal requirements placed upon teachers, what real freedom to respond to individuals remains? Discussion in Chapter 12 suggests that there is no blanket answer to this question and that we need to examine different aspects individually, and in terms of degree of possibility rather than all or nothing.
2.   To gain a clear understanding of, and feel for, the procedural principles involved in structuring and monitoring openly developing situations, as discussed in the previous two chapters.
3.   To develop strategies for the practical management of such situations and the organization of resources.

It seems to me that the poetic approach has both its advantages and its challenges in these practical respects. It will be helpful to outline these as a preliminary to looking at ways of approaching more specific practical problems.

The practical advantages of the poetic approach are as follows: the teacher is released from the stress involved in maintaining an appearance of being 'all-knowing' and totally 'in charge'; as children grow in confidence in their own thoughts and ideas, so the teacher is released from the mill of having to constantly provide them with inspiration; the teacher becomes a learner – a co-worker – with its concomitant satisfactions in terms of receiving from the situation as well as giving to it; children become less demanding of teacher time in terms of petty instructions as they learn to use their own initiative and take on more responsibility for their own learning. The main problems are, I think, a loss of the sense of security that a carefully pre-specified set of objectives can provide; the loss of convenience of pre-packaged schemes of work; the difficulty in anticipating, and therefore providing, relevant resources; anxieties about monitoring progress.

How are such problems to be overcome? Solutions are clearly going to be very context-specific, but perhaps the first thing to be said is that the poetic approach suggests a change of attitude towards the problems themselves. They become regarded less as obstacles to be overcome in order for learning to occur, and more as *sources of learning in themselves*. The notion of co-responsibility and working *with* children rather than *upon* them suggests that finding practical solutions to at least some of these problems is an integral part of developing children's thinking and that they therefore need to be brought into such decision-making. In this way they will be able to share the teacher's concerns and benefit from rich opportunities to develop their own practical judgement in matters which are of prime concern to them. In this way, too, their thinking can become rooted in the realities of situations where compromises have to be negotiated and responsible foresight and planning have to be exercised. With this in mind, let us consider some practical suggestions for enabling such co-responsibility and participation.

First, it will presumably be important for the teacher to have a clear idea of the likely practical opportunities and constraints under which the work will generally have to be undertaken – such things as availability of rooms and other school-based resources, notice needed to obtain material from the local library, to arrange day trips, etc. Second, it will be important to allow sufficient time for proper discussion and negotiation of the area of work itself, and for it to be properly resourced. While clearly, for the many reasons rehearsed throughout this book, it would be quite inappropriate to attempt to provide a universal procedure for the practical organization of such work, the following represents an example of but one such approach, and one that I have seen used to good effect with a class of 7- to 8-year-olds, which might be considered and adapted (or rejected!) according to circumstances.

Having established through discussion the general character of an enterprise in terms of its broad aspirations and content, the class might be divided into groups to consider in more detail their own interests, and the possible requirements of different elements in terms of skills and knowledge, time and resources. (They may well record their ideas in their own webs or flow diagrams, etc.) The results of these discussions could be brought back to the class as a whole for further evaluation in terms of their rationale and feasibility, and lists of preparatory tasks could be made with responsibility being assigned to appropriate individuals or groups. Depending on the extent of the enterprise, such preliminary discussions might take place before a weekend, or a shorter school holiday such as half-term or Christmas, so that there is proper opportunity for all involved to get together whatever is needed before the project proper gets under way. In this way everyone has the chance to develop a feel for the work and a responsible attitude towards it in terms of its demands and practical constraints. Of course, as new opportunities and problems arise during the progress of the work, solutions will need to be negotiated between the interested parties and compromises worked through. Throughout, the role of the teacher would be to support, provoke, challenge, in the ways previously discussed in order to enhance the quality of children's engagement and understanding.

But, can young children handle this? I suspect there can be no general answer to this. No doubt some will do so better than others and we must simply be careful not to make quick assumptions on the matter. There is certainly considerable evidence to suggest that even pre-school children can, given the right kind of support, engage in the procedures of 'plan, do, review' in quite a systematic way and thus take some explicit responsibility for the organization of their learning.[4] But whatever the possibilities here, all children need to learn to begin to take on such responsibility one way or another, and in degrees compatible with their capacities, if they are to begin to develop the qualities of thinking a genuinely free society demands. Of course many children exhibit precisely these qualities naturally enough and to a lesser or greater extent in play situations. Provided the attitude of the teacher is such that she rates the value of learning to discuss and negotiate, to exercise judgement and choice, to accept personal responsibility, i.e. to achieve a degree of authentic understanding, as being at least the equal to the learning of 'subject-matter', there seems to be every reason for extending this activity into the 'serious' work of the classroom. But, in truth, this way of speaking is itself now somewhat misleading. It is in danger of re-erecting the old dichotomy of child and subject-matter when the burden of what I have been trying to convey from the poetic perspective is the essential relationship between learner and what is to be learnt. It is an attempt to provide a reinterpretation of what it is to be a 'learner' and what *counts* as 'subject-matter', in a truly educational situation, which overcomes this dichotomy.

So now, to draw things to a conclusion: one of the central points about the poetic approach to teaching is that it provides a stance for dealing with problems which makes them the shared concern of both teacher and pupils, and works towards an openness in which they are resolved in ways which draw upon the ideas of all concerned. The resolution of arising problems through this kind of social relationship gives both a sense of ownership and responsibility to all involved and, very importantly, an increased likelihood of solutions which are genuinely tailored to the situation which they have to meet. In eschewing pre-specified perceptions of situations and stock answers, in listening to and freely responding to the subtle nuances of particular situations in the senses previously developed, the teacher is not thoughtlessly pursuing some impractical and irrelevant ideal, but facing up to reality in a fuller sense: the quality of *these* children's thinking in *this* situation, and the potential mystery and many-sidedness of the things and relationships that comprise it. How well she will cope with this reality will, as always, have to remain to be seen, but at least she and her pupils will be honestly attending to the truth of their situation. And, ultimately, there is no other path to secure the development of those central aspects of thinking and understanding which have been the concern of this book.

NOTES AND REFERENCES

1 I have also developed this idea in direct comparison with rationalist approaches to education in 'Personal authenticity and public standards', in Cooper (1986).
2 See, for example, Elliott and Adelman (1975).
3 For some further development of this claim, see M. Bonnett and C. Doddington. 'Primary teaching: what has philosophy to offer?', in Lofthouse (1991).
4 With regard to the capacity of pre-school children to work in this way see, for example, the work and publications of the High/Scope Institute, London. See also the interesting account given by Alistair Fraser (1987) of ways in which primary school children took an active part in broad areas of decision-making in his school, and the accounts of child-led project work given by Roger Revell (1987, 1988).

Poetic Thinking and Personal Authenticity

As characterized by the writers we have been considering, rational thinking achieves its rigour by the application of public rule-governed procedures to experience in terms of which it is thus organized and validated. In this way objectivity essentially becomes a function of agreed conventions, a function of the shared criteria for deciding how things are to be classified and what is to count as true. In contrast, it has been argued, the rigour of poetic thinking has a more demanding basis: the source of its discipline and objectivity is not an orthodoxy of this kind, but *adequacy to the thing being revealed*. This involves a unique subjective response, and thus, it will be suggested, in a certain sense a heightened sense of personal responsibility. The argument is difficult, but it is important from the point of view of establishing the overall position. It revolves around the notion that genuine openness to things as they are in themselves, as against perceiving objects defined by categories, involves *awareness of negation*. I will now try to spell this out a little.

The main point is that to see something in one way, to reveal it on one occasion, is always at the expense of other ways of seeing it, other possibilities of revealing. There are always sides of the thing to which we will not be attending, or are out of view. There are aspects that will always remain unknown and beyond our grasp but which are not any the less part of the thing itself. For example, and above all, its simple ability to stand there, to exist. Thus openness to the thing itself, in its fullness, involves an apprehension of denial – a sense of the ambience of what is incipiently present but not revealed as such in our current awareness of it. Only in this way can things have restored to them their inherent strangeness – which is essential to their own integrity. In this sense even the most familiar of things has its mysterious aspect.

We can sometimes experience something of this if we stare

intently at an object for a period of time, say a flower. In such an experience the public criterion-referenced properties in terms of which we classify it and it can be 'known' as a defined object can fall away, become less dominant. And in its place a sense of the flower's own presence – standing forth – as something essentially inscrutable with a quality we cannot adequately articulate, can strike us and inspire us with a sense of wonderment: an awareness of what simply *is*, arising out of what is *not*. For much of the time, of course, dominated by the need for goal-orientated action, such staring is a comparatively rare experience. We are too busy organizing things, and need for the most part to see them as instances of everyday categories which can be routinely manipulated. In this way we come to live predominantly with *objects* rather than *things*.

Now such awareness of negation is precisely what lies at the kernel of personal responsibility: an awareness of what one has denied in what one has achieved. For in a way that parallels the above, every achievement, too, is gained at the expense of other real possibilities; it involves the realization of certain options as against others which could have been taken up but which were passed by. It is only in the consciousness of such choice, awareness of such negation, that responsibility arises and a sense of guilt can be possible. In this sense, then, it is the same developed sense of finitude that comes into play in revealing the individuality and particularity of things themselves as is being engendered in the self-expression of individuals who are striving to live authentically in the existentialist sense. And thus, only true individuals can relate poetically, for the discipline and rigour of poetic awareness are rooted in this underlying sense of responsibility being applied towards the finitude of things in their present and particular standing out from what they are not. We could perceive, represent, create things differently, but we are always involved in a limited selection of the possibilities that are actually open. This is part of the nature of things and our own essential finitude in relation to them. This element in awareness differentiates it from simple 'childish' enthraldom.

Now this claim concerning the relationship between a developed sense of our own finitude and our capacity to reveal the individuality of things themselves has broader implications. It suggests that the development of thinking in its deepest and fullest sense will indeed involve initiation into the essence of the human condition in the way advocated by existentialism. Human finitude is most poignantly expressed in human *mortality*. As long as we are living, as against being caught up in some state of mental limbo characterized by inauthenticity, we are also dying. Sense of life, assertion – its felt urgency – is enabled by sense of death, denial. As poetry often tries to make explicit, joy in what is present occurs against the backcloth of sadness of what is past or lost or cannot be, and vice versa. This characterizes our situation and enables our way of revealing things, giving human awareness, receptiveness, and responsiveness, its own essential quality. An omnipotent god cannot experience things as humans do – cannot reveal things in the way humans do, nor share in their meaning the way humans do – because it lacks this sense of finitude. There is no finality in its life; it has unlimited time and unlimited power to undo and re-do. Whatever meaning it is capable of experiencing, it is not of a kind intelligible to humans. Humans are individualized by their sense of finitude: they *are* as individuals, as much in virtue of what they are not – what their individuality denies, negates – as in virtue of what their individuality positively expresses or enables. Awareness of finitude is not, then, awareness of nothing, but a remembrance of what is being forgotten when we sum things up in categories and attempt to order our lives and the world in terms of them.

Now the important upshot of all this is that fully-fledged authentic thinking is not egocentric, but acknowledges the negation which pervades whole-hearted human involvement. Responsible choice and decision are still present in poetic thinking – are essential to it, but the sense of responsibility is not now simply of the kind emphasized by the notion of self-referencing. It is not self-conscious deliberation, but a tacit responsibility towards a revealing relationship with the thing itself. We live richly, and think poetically, insofar as we reveal things in their fullness. This means a responding to what is there in its arising from what is not, and a sense of wonder that things *are*. In this apprehension lies poetic thinking's sense of *wholeness* of the world – its intuitive sense of the ground out of which things arise and in which they are rooted, which is quite different from the discursive sense of *interrelatedness* conveyed through the imposition of webs of rationally constructed categories upon it.

Bibliography

Adorno, T. (1986) *The Jargon of Authenticity*. London: Routledge & Kegan Paul.

Aronwitz, S. and Giroux, H. (1986) *Education under Siege*. London: Routledge & Kegan Paul.

Axline, V. (1966) *In Search of Self*. London: Gollancz.

Bailey, C. H. (1983) *Beyond the Present and the Particular: A Theory of Liberal Education*. London, Routledge & Kegan Paul.

Bailey, C. H. (1992) 'Enterprise and liberal education: a reply to David Bridges', *Journal of Philosophy of Education*, 26(1).

Bantock, G. H. (1952) *Freedom and Authority in Education*. London: Faber & Faber.

Barrett, W. (1978) 'Heidegger and modern existentialism'. In B. Magee, (ed.), *Men of Ideas*. London: BBC Publications.

Barrow, R. (1987) 'Skill talk', *Journal of Philosophy of Education*, 21(2).

Barrow, R. and Woods, R. (1990) *An Introduction to Philosophy of Education*. London: Routledge.

Bettelheim, B. (1976) *The Uses of Enchantment*. London: Thames & Hudson.

Bonnett, M. (1978) 'Authenticity and education', *Journal of Philosophy of Education*, 12.

Bonnett, M. (1983) 'Education in a destitute time', *Journal of Philosophy of Education*, 17(1).

Bonnett, M. (1986) 'Personal Authenticity and Public Standards'. In Cooper, D. (ed.) (1986).

Bonnett, M. and Doddington, C. (1991) 'Primary teaching: what has philosophy to offer?' In Lofthouse, B. (ed.) (1991).

Bottery, M. (1990) *The Morality of the School*. London: Cassell.

Bridges, D. (1988) *Education, Democracy and Discussion*. Lanham: University Press of America.

Bridges, D. (1992) 'Enterprise and liberal education', *Journal of Philosophy of Education*, 26(1).

Cassirer, E. (1925) *Language and Myth*, translated by S. K. Langer (1946). New York: Harper.

Conner, C. (1988) 'Learning styles and classroom practice'. In Conner, C. (ed.) (1988).

Conner, C. (ed.) (1988) *Topic and Thematic Work in the Primary and Middle Years*. Cambridge Institute of Education.

Cooper, D. (1983) *Authenticity and Learning*. London: Routledge & Kegan Paul.

Cooper, D. (ed.) (1986) *Education, Values and Mind*. London: Routledge & Kegan Paul.

Dadds, M. (1988) 'Whose learning is it anyway? Concern about continuity and control in topic work'. In Conner, C. (ed.) (1988).

Davidson, M. (1969) *Helen Keller's Teacher*. London: Macdonald & Janes.

Dearden, R. F. (1967) 'Learning through discovery and learning through instruction'. In Peters, R. S. (ed.) (1967) *The Concept of Education*. London: Routledge & Kegan Paul.

Dearden, R. F., Hirst, P. H., and Peters, R. S. (eds) (1972) *Education and the Development of Reason*. London: Routledge & Kegan Paul.

DES (1988) *Task Group on Assessment and Testing: A Report*. London: HMSO.

DES (1991a) *Science in the National Curriculum*. London: HMSO.

DES (1991b) *Mathematics in the National Curriculum*. London: HMSO.

Dewey, J. (1902) *The Child and the Curriculum*. Reprinted in Dewey, J. (1956) *The Child and the Curriculum and The School and Society*. London: University of Chicago Press.

Dewey, J. (1933) *How We Think* (revised ed.). Boston: Heath.

Dunlop, F. (1984) *The Education of Feeling and Emotion*. London: George Allen & Unwin.

Egan, K. (1990) *Romantic Understanding*. London: Routledge.

Elliott, J. and Adelman, C. (1975) 'Aspirations into reality', *Education 3–13*, **3**(2).

Elliott, R. K. (1975) 'Education and human being'. In Brown, S. C. (ed.) (1975) *Philosophers Discuss Education*. London: Macmillan.

Fraser, A. (1987) 'A child-structured learning context', *Cambridge Journal of Education*, **17**(3).

Frowe, I. (1992) 'Persuasive forces: language, ideology, and education'. In Andrews, R. (ed.) (1992) *The Rebirth of Rhetoric: Essays in Language, Culture and Education*. London: Routledge.

Heidegger, M. (1927) *Being and Time*, translated by J. Macquarrie and E. Robinson (1962). Oxford: Basil Blackwell.

Heidegger, M. (1943) 'On the essence of truth'. In Krell, D. F. (ed.) (1978) *Martin Heidegger: Basic Writings*. London: Routledge & Kegan Paul.

Heidegger, M. (1954a) *What Is Called Thinking?* translated by J. Glenn Gray (1968). New York: Harper & Row.

Heidegger, M. (1954b) 'The Question Concerning Technology'. In Heidegger, M. (1977).

Heidegger, M. (1969) *Discourse on Thinking*, translated by J. M. Anderson and E. H. Freund. New York: Harper & Row.

Heidegger, M. (1971) *Poetry, Language, Thought*, translated by A. Hofstadter. New York: Harper & Row.

Bibliography

Heidegger, M. (1977) *The Question Concerning Technology and Other Essays*, translated by W. Lovitt. New York: Harper & Row.

Hirst, P. H. (1965) 'Liberal education and the nature of knowledge'. In Archambault, R. D. (1965) *Philosophical Analysis and Education*. London: Routledge & Kegan Paul.

Hirst, P. H. (1993) 'The Foundations of the National Curriculum: Why Subjects?' In O'Hear, P. and White, J. (eds) (1993) *Assessing the National Curriculum*. London: Paul Chapman.

Hirst, P. H. and Peters, R. S. (1972) *The Logic of Education*. London: Routledge & Kegan Paul.

Holt, J. (1990) *How Children Fail* (2nd ed.). Harmondsworth: Penguin Books.

Ibsen, H. (1866) *Brand*, translated by M. Meyer (1973). London: Rupert Hart-Davis.

Kierkegaard, S. (1843) *Fear and Trembling and Sickness Unto Death*, translated by W. Lowrie (1970). Princeton, New Jersey: Princeton University Press.

Kreuger, F. (1926) 'The essence of feeling'. In Arnold, M. (1968) *The Nature of Emotion*. Harmondsworth: Penguin Books.

Lawrence, D. H. (1923) 'Benjamin Franklin'. Reprinted in Williams, J. and Williams, R. (eds) (1973).

Lawrence, D. H. (1936) 'Education of the people'. Reprinted in Williams, J. and Williams, R. (eds) (1973).

Lofthouse, B. (ed.) (1991) *The Study of Primary Education: A Source Book*, 1. London: Falmer Press.

Manley Hopkins, G. (1979) *The Major Poems*, edited by W. Davies. London: J. M. Dent.

Matthews, G. (1980) *Philosophy and the Young Child*. Cambridge, Mass: Harvard University Press.

Mill, J. S. (1859) 'On Liberty'. Reprinted in Mill, J. S. *Utilitarianism, Liberty and Representative Government* (1971) London: J. M. Dent.

Murray, M. (1978) *Heidegger and Modern Philosophy*. London: Yale University Press.

Murris, M. (1992) *Teaching Philosophy with Picture Books*. London: Infonet.

NCC (1989) *Curriculum Guidance One: A Framework for the Primary Curriculum*. York: National Curriculum Council.

Nietzsche, F. (1889) *The Twilight of the Idols*, translated by R. J. Hollingdale (1981). Harmondsworth: Penguin Books.

Oakeshott, M. (1972) 'Education: the engagement and its frustration'. In Dearden, R. F. *et al.* (eds) (1972).

Peters, R. S. (1966) *Ethics and Education*. London: Allen & Unwin.

Peters, R. S. (1970) 'The education of the emotions'. In Dearden, R. F. *et al.* (eds) (1972).

Peters, R. S. (1972) 'Reason and passion'. In Dearden, R. F. *et al.* (eds) (1972).

Peters, R.S. (1974) 'Subjectivity and standards'. In Peters, R.S. (1974) *Psychology and Ethical Development*. London: Allen & Unwin.

Pole, D. (1972) 'The concept of reason'. In Dearden, R.F. *et al.* (eds) (1972).

Revell, R. (1987) 'Travelling Baedeker-less', *Cambridge Journal of Education*, **17**(3).

Revell, R. (1988) 'Where Goldie Sleeps . . .' In Conner, C. (ed.) (1988).

Robins, K. and Webster, F. (1989) *The Technical Fix*. London: Macmillan.

Rousseau, J.-J. (1762) *Emile*. In Boyd, W. (1975) *Emile for Today: The Emile of Jean-Jacques Rousseau*. London: Heinemann.

Ryle, G. (1949) *The Concept of Mind*. London: Hutchinson.

Sartre, J.-P. (1943) *Being and Nothingness*, translated by H. Barnes (1957). London: Methuen.

Sartre, J.-P. (1965) *Literature and Existentialism* (3rd ed.). New York: Citadel Press.

Schiller, C. (1946) 'The assessment of the attainment of young children'. In Schiller, C. (1979) *Christian Schiller: In His Own Words*. London: A. & C. Black for National Association for Primary Education.

Smith, F. (1992) *To Think: in Language, Learning and Education*. London: Routledge.

Smith, R. (1987) 'Skills: the middle way', *Journal of Philosophy of Education*, **21**(2).

Standish, P. (1992) *Beyond the Self*. Aldershot: Avebury.

Stenhouse, L. (1971) 'The Humanities Curriculum Project: The rationale', *Theory into Practice*, **10**(3).

Stenhouse, L. (1975) *Introduction to Curriculum Research and Development*. London: Heinemann.

Styles, M., Bearne, E. and Watson, V. (eds) (1992) *After Alice*. London: Cassell.

Watson, V. (1992) 'Irresponsible writers and responsible readers'. In Styles, M. *et al.* (eds) (1992).

White, J.P. (1973) *Towards a Compulsory Curriculum*. London: Routledge & Kegan Paul.

White, J.P. (1982) *The Aims of Education Restated*. London: Routledge & Kegan Paul.

Whitehead, A.N. (1932) 'The aims of education'. Reprinted in *The Aims of Education and Other Essays* (1966). London: Ernest Benn.

Williams, J. and Williams, R. (eds) (1973) *D.H. Lawrence on Education*. Harmondsworth: Penguin Books.

Wittgenstein, L. (1958) *Philosophical Investigations*. Oxford: Basil Blackwell.

Name Index

Adelman, C. 189n
Adorno, T. 107n
Aristotle 31
Axline, V. 117n

Bacon, F. 135
Bailey, C. 11n, 66-72, 75-6,
    81, 84, 92, 120, 126
Baker, K. 28
Bantock, G. 143n
Barrett, W. 138
Barrow, R. 31, 40n
Bettelheim, B. 117n
Bonnett, M. 117n, 127n
Bottery, M. 11n, 127n
Bridges, D. 11n, 163n

Carroll, L. 51
Cassirer, E. 39n
Conner, C. 163n
Cooper, D. 127n

Dadds, M. 12n
Darwin, C. 84, 87

Davidson, M. 38n
Dearden, R. 40n, 65, 85
Descartes 3
Dewey, J. 26-7, 153
Doddington, C. 189n
Drummond, W. 31
Dunlop, F. 21n

Egan, K. 21n
Einstein, A. 84
Elliott, J. 189n
Elliott, R.K. 127n

Fraser, A. 189n
Frowe, I. 11n

Giroux, H. 12n

Heidegger, M. 98, 101-3,
    105-6, 125, 129, 131-3,
    136, 141
Hepburn, R.W. 20n

Subject Index

202